John Marsden was born in 1950, the third of four children. His life has been colourful and varied: everything from working in abattoirs and pizza shops, to four years as Head of English at Geelong Grammar's famous Timbertop campus.

In 1987 John's first book was published, and since then he has become one of Australia's best-known and most popular authors.

Novels like *Letters from the Inside* and *Tomorrow, When the War Began*, and the writing manual *Everything I Know About Writing*, have earned him sales of over a million copies in Australia, and many more overseas.

John now lives just outside Melbourne, on a thousand acre bush property, where he runs writing workshops for groups of young people and adults.

Also by John Marsden

So Much to Tell You
The Journey
The Great Gatenby
Staying Alive in Year 5
Out of Time
Letters from the Inside
Take My Word for It
Looking for Trouble
Tomorrow . . . (Ed.)
Cool School
Creep Street
Checkers
For Weddings and a Funeral (Ed.)
This I Believe (Ed.)
Dear Miffy
Prayer for the 21st Century
Everything I Know About Writing
Secret Men's Business
The *Tomorrow* Series 1999 Diary
The Rabbits
Norton's Hut
Marsden on Marsden
Winter
The Head Book
The Boy You Brought Home
The Magic Rainforest
Millie
A Roomful of Magic

The *Tomorrow* Series
Tomorrow, When the War Began
The Dead of the Night
The Third Day, the Frost
Darkness, Be My Friend
Burning for Revenge
The Night is for Hunting
The Other Side of Dawn

The Ellie Chronicles
While I Live
Incurable
Circle of Flight

secret men's business

manhood: the big gig

john marsden

First published 1998 in Pan by Pan Macmillan Australia Pty Limited
1 Market Street, Sydney

Reprinted 1998 (twice), 1999, 2000, 2003, 2004, 2006, 2010, 2011

National Library of Australia
Cataloguing-in-Publication data:

Marsden, John, 1950–
Secret men's business

ISBN 978 0 330 36074 6

1. Men – Conduct of life. 2. Men – Psychology. I. Title.

646.70081

Typeset in 11/15 pt New Aster by Post Pre-Press Group, Brisbane
Printed by IVE

Dedicated to David Loader,
a good man and a good friend

ACKNOWLEDGEMENTS

Thanks to the many who have given me ideas, stories, or things to think about over the years; specifically, in the case of this book, Noelene Horton, Nick Lillie, Bruno Bettelheim, Michael Schwartz, Alice Miller, Antoinette Ryan, David Loader, Rosalind Alexander, and thousands of others.

The author would like to acknowledge that small portions of this text have appeared in *Everything I Know About Writing* (Reed, 1993) and *The Written World*, edited by Agnes Nieuwenhuizen (Thorpe, 1994).

BECOMING A MAN: The Big Gig

Becoming a man is the biggest challenge you'll ever have.

There are 12 things you need to do, if you are to reach manhood.

Of course in one way all you have to do to become a man is to stay alive. Physically you will grow into a man.

As you reach different birthdays you'll be given some of the 'tickets' of adulthood, whether you're ready or not.

So, at 18 you'll be allowed to drink alcohol, even if you have an emotional age of six. You'll be able to vote at 18, even if you think Humphrey B. Bear is President of the U.S.A. and Canberra is a brand of salami.

You'll be allowed to go to R-rated films,

although your ideas of sex might be based on what you've read on toilet walls, and you think violence is a good way to communicate with other people. After a few tests you'll be able to drive a car, even if you are vicious and irresponsible.

But to become a man who is mature, independent, responsible and wise you'll need to do a little more than just stay alive and have birthdays.

It's worth going for it though. There are a lot of good things about being a man, including . . .

- You take control of your own life
- You can protect others
- People look to you for leadership
- You can make things happen
- You can reshape the world, on a small scale – for example, by building your own house or becoming a youth worker; or on a big scale – for example, by producing a movie that's a huge international hit
- You can help others
- A whole new world of interesting experiences opens up for you

One of the reasons it's difficult to become a man is that you are encouraged in so many ways to remain immature. Schools, and some parents, want to keep you as a child. They feel you will be easier to control if you are still a child, that you will be more 'biddable' (more likely to do what you're told). They might not want to acknowledge the fact that you are now sexually potent. Your father may have been the only sexually potent male in the house up until now, and he could feel threatened.

One of the ways this might show is by his teasing you about girls, or about your first dates. It is cruel to tease you about something you probably already feel anxious about, but it shows that he's got mixed feelings about your maturing.

He may even flirt with your girlfriend or show too much curiosity about your activities with girls. This is not appropriate, nor is it helpful. You will need to show more dignity and maturity than him in this situation, and maybe arrange your life so you have more privacy.

On the other hand your father may feel proud of the new stage you have reached, and pleased that your relationship with him is on a new and more mature level. Many men are more comfortable with their sons when they can talk on a more equal level.

In this situation if he teases you occasionally, you know it's part of the affectionate relationship you have. You'll probably give as good as you get.

Your mother could be nervous that there is now another sexually potent male in the house, and she may try to keep you as her 'little boy' for a while longer, so she can keep mothering you. In this situation she wants to deny your growth. This is not in your best long-term interests.

On the other hand she could be delighted by your new-found independence and maturity. She might be pleased by the fact that she can now have more time to follow her own interests.

Another reason it can be difficult to become a man is that you are yourself nervous of growing up. If you have a loving mother and/or father, leaving their constant care and protection can be hard. Having to take on adult concerns and responsibilities mightn't appear like too good a gig.

Adults always look so worried. They complain loudly and often of how tough it is to be an adult, with job worries, mortgage repayments, relationship difficulties. They tell you how easy it is for kids. Their eyes mist over as they recall the magical stress-free days of their childhood, the 'happiest days of their life'.

They have short memories.

I talked to a group of Year 10 students once about these issues. I was surprised at the large number who said they were in no hurry to grow up; that from where they stood, adult life didn't look good at all.

I wanted to say to them: 'Well, I've done both, and believe me, being an adult leaves being a kid for dead.'

But although that was my experience it might not necessarily be theirs. There was no point forcing my experiences onto them. So instead I talked about the advantages of being an adult: how you can make your own decisions, have greater freedom, have access to a wider range of activities, earn your own money, travel more widely.

Despite that, I'm well aware that there are many adults who never grow up. They cause problems for themselves and others. It is certain that you know a number of adults in this category.

Actor Omar Sharif once said to an interviewer on television: 'I've never met a man who's really grown up. Have you?'

My first thought was to say to Omar, 'You need to get out more.' That's still what I'd say to him today. But I have to admit that I can't think of too many men whom I'd call 'grown up'.

Perhaps this helps explain some of the discontent women have felt about men over the years. Perhaps they have had good reason to feel upset, although of course there are plenty of women who don't grow up either.

Here's a few generalisations we can make about immature men. They place too much emphasis on sport. They run away from anything serious. They throw tantrums when they don't get their own way. They tell crude, sexist or racist jokes. They blame everything that goes wrong on everyone and everything else. They expect the government to fix their lives for them. They treat women in a patronising or contemptuous way (probably the same way they treated their mothers). They run away from the responsibilities of fathering. In fact they run away from responsibilities generally. They waste money on childish things, toys, like spoilers for their car or subwoofers for their maxi-blasters.

They dream of someone dropping an enormous amount of money into their lap, so that they don't have to work any more. They are jealous of other people's successes. If they have children they favour and spoil one at the expense of others.

They drive dangerously, handle alcohol and drugs inappropriately, cheat on their partners and their families, undermine other important adults in your life and want to talk to you about matters that are none of your business, like problems between them and their partner.

They hero-worship other men, agreeing with everything they say, putting themselves at their beck and call and laughing for half an hour every time their hero makes a joke. They let other people, like the boss at work, walk all over them, and although they complain bitterly about it, they don't seem able to take appropriate action. They're often extremely angry. Road rage is a classic symptom of immaturity in men.

If this is the kind of adult you want to be, the kind of man you want to grow into, then don't bother reading this book. Go back to writing on toilet walls, telling jokes about the size of women's vaginas, doing drugs and alcohol, and putting crap on people who are more focused, purposeful and mature than you.

On the other hand this book can help you become the kind of man you secretly, or openly, want to be.

It's not easy. There are a lot of obstacles in the way. I was at a school the other day where a teacher had given the Year 8 students the assignment of writing a poem which began with the words 'I am a child who . . .'

I wondered at his choice of topic. It seems to me that students in Year 8 are not children any longer. I wondered if the teacher was trying to force onto them the view that they were still children. Maybe he was more comfortable dealing with children, and wanted to keep them in that role.

Many adults hold a view that children are sweet little angels who respect adults and will do whatever they're told. (They get very angry, incidentally, when children don't behave like this.) They don't want children to grow up into those nasty teenagers who talk too loudly and challenge rules and want their own lives.

I think another thing that makes it hard for boys to grow up is the constant message that immaturity is attractive, and maturity boring.

This message is regularly given to us by two of the most powerful media in the world today – American movies and American television. Children in these programmes act like adults, and we are expected to find it cute and appealing. Teenagers behave in ways that are gross and disgusting and we are expected to find that funny. And adults act like infants.

Or, in a bizarre twist on this, the children and teenagers act like parents, and the parents act like children.

An airline magazine describes the movie *House Arrest* in these words: 'A teenage boy and his young sister, learning that their parents plan to separate, lock them in the basement hoping the couple will resolve their problems. Three of their friends think it's such a good idea that they too lure their parents to the house and lock them up. All the parents are kept under house arrest while the children give them therapy sessions and rule the roost.'

A newspaper review of *Curly Sue* says: 'An orphan cons a lawyer into letting her and her guardian move in with her, then uses all her charms to spark a romance between the two.'

The child is running both adults' lives for them.

The movie *What about Bob?* has a hero who is an adult but acts like a three-year-old. He is a monstrous person, infantile, self-obsessed, a liar, and unable to respect limits. His psychiatrist is self-obsessed too, but the message is that we'll all be better people if we can just be like Bob.

Children and teenagers in these films advise their parents on how they should conduct themselves on dates, whom they should (re)marry, how they should acquire confidence and self-esteem. Audiences are expected to break into uncontrollable gooey sighs and mop their eyes with tissues, as these lines, written by cynical adults for the child stars, are uttered.

Ironically, many of the child stars who utter these wise lines have their own lives destroyed by their movie and television careers.

Giving advice on dating, on confidence and self-esteem, on marriage, is the role of parents, not cute Hollywood 10-year-old stars. In some cultures parents even have the vital role of telling young people whom they should marry.

Growing up can be extra difficult for the sons of highly successful parents. They often get confused between their parents' achievements and their own. So, for example, I hear them boasting about their Porsche, their holiday house, their overseas trip. They don't seem to realise that these are their parents' achievements, bought with money they've earned. In no sense can the son of the family take credit for these possessions.

It's especially important for young men in highly successful families to have achievements they can truly call their own. A school principal told me of a Duke of Edinburgh Gold Award Scheme hike that some students from her school undertook. This would have been a good example of a major achievement that the students could truly and proudly call their own. Yet their parents destroyed it by meeting them at several points along the way with Eskies of food and cold drinks.

The principal who told me this story said the parents were 'well-meaning'. I don't agree. I think their motives were quite complex, but were more to do with their desire to possess their children in an inappropriate way, to intrude on their lives.

On the other hand I remember a young man from a powerful and wealthy Canberra family who was having massive behaviour problems and had been expelled from a number of schools. At the age of 16 he was introduced to rock climbing. At his first attempt he astonished his teacher by his ability. He went on to become one of Australia's best climbers, leaving his family in awe at his achievements.

So this book is not about excuses. I don't want to spend the whole book telling you of the obstacles to your becoming an adult. Let it be said of you, as it was once said of British doctor Jonathan Miller: 'Obstacles are a stimulus to him.'

What a compliment!

In the past, in some societies, the outward signs of reaching manhood have been things like having sex with a woman, going to war, killing an animal.

These are powerful events which can have a big impact. If you feel that it is important for you to experience them as you move into adulthood, here are some points to consider:

1. Sex with a woman: obviously the best way to have sex is in a loving mature relationship, where both people are committed and there for the long term.

Sex is an act with big implications. If you think it's on the same level as watching TV or playing table tennis, you're missing the meaning. You haven't got much idea of what's going on.

But if you want to have sex with a woman as some kind of conquest, that you think will make you a man, better you should go to a brothel than take advantage of a girl you know. To have sex with someone you know, pretending you care for her when in fact you just want to 'collect' her as a 'trophy', is an act completely lacking in integrity and honesty.

Most Australian states now have legal brothels.

These can be found in the Yellow Pages under Adult Products and Services. Not all places listed are brothels. Some for example are escort services. Common sense will usually tell you which ones are brothels.

Brothels can be recognised in the street by the fact that most have pink, crimson or scarlet lighting or decorations, and names like 'Temptation' or 'Club X'.

The minimum age for males going to brothels is 18. The average cost for intercourse is $100. Condoms must be worn, and these are supplied by the brothel. Appointments need not be made. You simply turn up. The usual procedure is that you'll be invited into an area where you won't see other clients and they won't see you. Several women, perhaps three or four, will come out, and you'll be invited to choose one. She will then take you to a room where you have to wash your genitals and put on a condom. Kissing is not usually part of the deal, but the woman will make it clear what the limits are: respect what she says and act with courtesy at all times.

If you think there is a reasonable chance that you are gay, don't put yourself under unnecessary pressure by attempting this experience.

2. Going to war: you can join the Army Reserve at the age of 17. They give you full military training,

at weekends and during live-in camps. If you join, you have to attend for at least 14 days a year, but most members do more than that: on average, 40–50 days a year. You will be paid at least $65 a day tax free, and an extra $24 a day when you're out 'in the field' doing training exercises.

If you have a job your employer has to allow you time for Army Reserve activities.

If Australia goes to war, or if the government decides you are needed, members of the Army Reserve are ordered to join the full-time Army immediately, and are not allowed to refuse.

There are also Naval and Air Force Reserves.

You can get more information on the Army, Naval and Air Force Reserves by calling 13 19 02.

3. Killing an animal: I would suggest that killing an animal with a rifle is weak. Especially if you use a high-powered rifle, or a rifle with telescopic sights. It is cheating, because you are not using your natural skills: you are using the technology of the rifle manufacturer. Under those circumstances a six-year-old could kill the animal.

The only genuine hunting for land animals is that done with traditional weapons, like a bow and arrow. It is still quite high-tech, because modern bows and arrows are pretty sophisticated. But you will actually have to use your own skills. You will have to stalk the animal. It will be extremely difficult. But if you succeed, your achievement will mean something.

For further information, try under Archery in the Yellow Pages.

Given the need to help our native fauna, who are under threat in so many ways, I suggest that your only legitimate prey in Australia today are feral and imported animals: rabbits, foxes, cats, pigs. I personally don't believe that duck shooting is an honourable activity, if only because of the number of rare and protected birds that are accidentally shot each year by duck hunters.

You should not go after pigs unless you have vast experience. Wild pigs are extremely savage. They can and do kill humans.

Incidentally, the above comments do not of course apply to farmers who use rifles to get rid of vermin: hunting in that situation has a totally different meaning.

Another way of killing animals is through fishing. Again, using technology to make the hunting easy, so it's almost impossible to fail, is cheating. It robs the activity of its meaning.

I suggest that fly-fishing is the truest form of fishing available nowadays. It requires skill, cunning, and is active, not passive. There is no sitting in a boat or on a jetty with your line in the water, half asleep, when you fly-fish. Fly-fishing is a craft.

You will need someone to teach you fly-fishing, and if you don't know anyone, the Yellow Pages, under Angling, or fishing shops like the 'Compleat Angler' chain will help you.

Of course if you're fishing for fun, or to get food, by all means go down to the jetty, or out in a boat. That's perfectly legitimate. It depends again on the reasons you have for the activity.

If you don't have access to the country for hunting, or the water for fishing, you might get enough satisfaction just by joining a rifle or pistol club, and shooting on a range at targets. These clubs can be found in all major cities. Look in the Yellow Pages under Gun Clubs.

The three activities discussed above – having sex with a woman, going to war, killing an animal – may, as I say, be very powerful. But they have never, in any society, been the full story when it comes to being a man. In fact you may consider that they are no longer meaningful or appropriate in the modern world. In the real, deepest sense of the word 'adult' they are meaningless.

Here instead are the 12 ways to reach adulthood in our society. Don't panic as you read them. You don't have to do all these things today or tomorrow. The time will come when something deep inside you tells you 'I should do this now'.

Listen to that voice and respect it.

On the other hand you may be ready for a number of these things now:

1. You Need To Defeat Your Father

This may not be necessary for young men who have excellent relationships with their fathers: relationships of mutual respect, liking and understanding.

Most teenage boys however need to defeat their fathers.

I remember talking to a group of 17-year-old males a few years ago. Several of them told stories of how they found themselves in a position to defeat their fathers for the first time.

One boy described racing his father along the beach. After a while he realised that his father was puffing and panting, falling further and further behind, no longer able to keep up. Until that moment the father had always been faster than his son.

Another told how he was playing his father at tennis. Suddenly he was serving at 5–1, 40–15, one point away from his first win over his father.

I asked the tennis player: 'What happened?'

He said: 'I double-faulted, lost that game and the next five, and lost the match 5–7.'

I asked the runner: 'Did the same thing happen to you? Did you fall over? Did you slow down and lose the race?'

'No way,' he said. 'I beat the bastard by the biggest margin I could.'

It seems to me that the second teenager might do better in the next stage of his life, because when the moment came he found the courage to go on and beat his father. He was ready to become a strong and independent adult.

The moment will come for you, if it hasn't already, when you realise you have surpassed your father in an area which is important and powerful for you both. You may realise you are now faster than your father or stronger or fitter. Not necessarily in a physical way either. It may be that you can at last beat him at chess, or use the computer more effectively, or do calculations in your head faster than he can.

You have to defeat him in a field in which you have always thought him to be superior: the acknowledged powerful one in the family in that particular area.

It may be that you can already use the computer better than he can, but it doesn't mean a huge amount if he didn't have great skills in that area to begin with.

A French writer tells the story of a boy who was dominated by his vain and ignorant father. The boy was not doing well at school. The father was angry when he saw the boy's reports and said: 'Right, from now on I'm going to take a hand in your education.'

A few days later the boy brought home his next

assignment, an essay. The father was very excited. 'I'll help you with this!' he said. 'Here, write down what I tell you.'

He dictated the entire essay to his son.

The boy took it to school the next day and handed it in as his own work.

Every day from then on his father asked him: 'Have you got the essay back yet? What did we get?'

Every day the boy answered: 'No, not yet father. They haven't been marked yet.'

Eventually however the great day came. The teacher handed out the essays. The last one on the pile was the boy's. The teacher held it up in front of the whole class.

'As for this essay,' he said to the students, 'in all my 22 years of teaching, I have never marked a more self-indulgent, badly written heap of absolute rubbish.'

That afternoon the boy came home again. Again the father was eagerly waiting. 'Have you got the essay back yet? What did we get?'

'Yes', said the boy. 'The teacher has marked them and we got them back today.'

'Well', asked the impatient man. 'Come on, tell me. What did he say?'

The boy stood there, trembling. It is the critical moment in the story. The reader understands that it's the critical moment in the boy's life. He can break his father's tyrannical hold over him forever, and begin to become his own person. Or he will be dominated by his father forever.

'The teacher said it was a wonderful essay,' he mumbled, 'and he gave it an A.'

'Good', says the father, rubbing his hands with glee. 'Now, what's the next topic? Come and sit down and we'll get started.'

Even where there is a positive relationship between father and son most young men still need to defeat their fathers.

Why?

Because for most boys, when they're little, their father seems so big and powerful that he is like a king. Everything the boy can do, the father can do better. The father is stronger, smarter, tougher.

The time comes to move on. If you grow up still thinking your father is bigger and dominant, you'll have an immature view of the world. More importantly, you'll feel you can never do better than him. He's always going to be Number One. The best you can hope for is to be Number Two. This is injurious to your confidence, and your development.

You have to recognise that not only is your father far from perfect, you're actually your own person. You have strengths and skills that are uniquely yours. Very different from your father's.

By defeating him you free yourself to go on and achieve the great things that life holds in store for you.

Some fathers think it is a good idea to deliberately make mistakes and let their sons beat them. They pretend they've foolishly put their queen in a bad position in a game of chess, or they hit a simple catch to you, or they pitch you a soft ball so you can hit a homer. This is not helpful. The son is left not knowing whether his victory is genuine, but suspecting it isn't. Worse, when he finally does achieve a real victory over his father, he's not convinced it is genuine.

You can tell a lot about your father and your relationship with him by the way he reacts to being beaten. A good father will smile, congratulate his son, be proud of his son's achievement. That shows greatness on his part. After all, it has been a powerful moment for him too. He has been brought face to face with his mortality. The young buck has beaten him. He is growing old. He may have known unconsciously that he was slowing down, getting weaker, but now he knows it for sure. Father Time has tapped him on the shoulder.

The good son will be sensitive to his father's feelings, and will not brag about his victory. But he may well celebrate it in a way that has meaning for him, and good on him too.

The bad father is angry at losing. He may be furious, and he shows it. The son's moment of victory is spoilt, and he is left wondering whether it really was a victory after all. The father has robbed this important moment of much of its meaning.

In one family I know the father collapsed, holding his heart. A doctor rushed to the scene. He could find nothing wrong and suggested that perhaps it was heat exhaustion.

Some boys reading this have no fathers. Some men reading this will feel that they never defeated their fathers at anything, or if they did the father rendered the victory hollow. They worry that now it's too late: the moment when it should have happened is long past.

Certainly it is hard to beat the absent father; of course literally it is impossible. But it can be done symbolically. I suggest you set out to do or make something which will represent your victory over your father. Choose something difficult, but something you will do supremely well. It might be a carving, a tough hike, a level of sporting achievement, the creation of a piece of music, the reconstruction of a car engine. It could be in a field where your father valued his own prowess, but it doesn't have to be.

Let your success be your victory over your missing father.

2. Leave School, Leave Home

It is impossible to reach manhood while you're still at school. There is no school that allows its students to become adults while they're still within the confines of the school.

This is a terrible statement to have to make about schools, and perhaps it's an issue you could address while you're still at your school. Perhaps you could help redesign the operations of the school.

While you're at school it's a good idea to sign up for as much work experience as possible, as, if the placements are right, you'll be in a mature environment with adults who will give you a realistic sense of life in the workplace.

As you know, however, most students feel they need to stay at school so they can eventually get the job they want. Then, when they leave secondary school, they may feel they have to go on to a tertiary college or university. On and on and on, until they're 22 or 23 or even older.

It's very difficult to reach maturity at tertiary colleges too, because the atmosphere continues to be childish, and no-one is likely to be interested in encouraging you to take on adult roles.

There is a solution, and that is to 'leave' after the final year of secondary school. In other words, to take at least a year to do other things. Not 'a year off' in the sense of being a slob for a year, doing nothing of any importance or meaning.

It doesn't mean doing what your parents direct you into either. By all means listen to your parents' advice, if they are people who listen to you, are sensitive to you, treat you with respect. But it's up to you to decide how to spend the year or years. Some possibilities include getting a job, travelling within Australia or overseas, doing something creative in the arts field or taking on volunteer work that will help others or help the environment.

Another way to leave school is to apply for one of the many exchange schemes available now for students to go overseas for a term or more of schooling. In a new environment, away from your parents, your friends, your own school, you'll need real strength of character, but you'll have many powerful new experiences.

Once you've left school, you should be thinking about leaving home too.

In normal circumstances you should not still be at home by the time you reach your twenties.

Time and time again I meet young people whom I used to teach. So often they're still living at home with their parents, and so often they hate it. 'It drives me crazy!' they say. 'If my mother makes one more comment about my hair . . . or my father tells me one more time to . . .'

I interrupt. 'Why don't you move out?'

'I can't afford to' is their invariable answer.

Of course they can afford to. What they mean

is, they're scared to move out. For at least three reasons: one, because they don't want to accept a poorer standard of living. They might even have to interrupt their studies for a while and earn some money to support themselves. This would be far better for them than staying on at home, but they're reluctant to do it.

Another reason, which they may not admit even to themselves, is that they don't feel confident about being away from their parents. And another is that they are scared of their parents' reaction to the idea.

Although parents may oppose your leaving home at first, in time even they might admit it's for the best. Too bad if they don't. Leave anyway.

Good parents take quite a different point of view. They recognise when the time has come for you to leave, and they encourage and support you in your decision. They might help you look for suitable accommodation, and lend you their spare furniture. If you're lucky they might even buy you a housewarming present.

Of course when you leave home it doesn't mean you leave your parents forever. There are three paths your life can take:

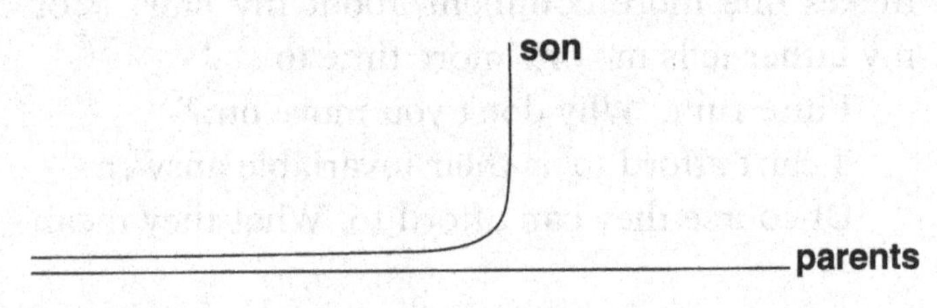

1. At adolescence the son goes in one direction and the parents go in another. They have almost no contact. This is not a healthy model.

son

parents

2. The son stays locked to the parents forever; not able to become his own person.

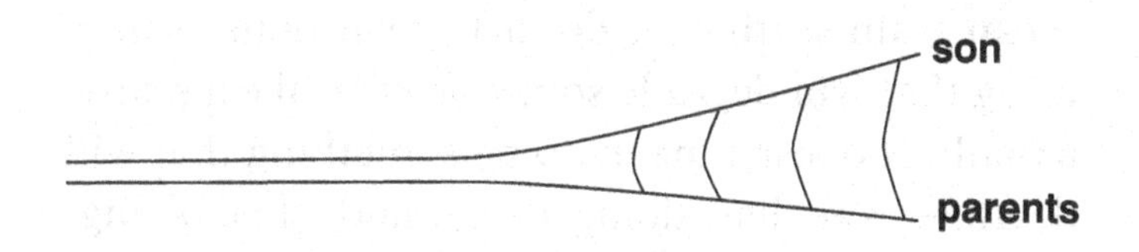

3. At adolescence the son starts to follow his own path, but keeps a good healthy relationship with his parents. This is of course the only valid way to go.

If your parents can afford it, or if you win a scholarship, a year or more at boarding school might be worth considering. That's one way you can 'leave home' while you're still at school. Another way is doing an exchange. It doesn't have to be overseas. It could be a city–country exchange, or an interstate exchange.

For your next birthday or Christmas ask your parents for a suitcase or two. Even if you're quite young. Start to prepare them now for the realisation that you're going to be moving out in a few years . . . or sooner.

3. You Need To Test And Demonstrate Your Courage

'Take care' is advice commonly offered. It can be good advice, but it can be a bit weak.

Sometimes the best advice is to 'take risks'.

'Taking risks' doesn't mean driving down the wrong side of the road at 140ks an hour. It doesn't mean train-surfing. It doesn't mean doing something that will degrade someone else, like a sexual assault. It doesn't mean doing something that will degrade you, like doing drugs and alcohol big-time. Not only are these things destructive, and self-destructive, they're lacking in creativity. They are activities without soul, without spirit, engaged in by young men struggling to find meaning in their lives.

In Australia one way you can test yourself is by going out into the natural environment. With the bush, the mountains, the coast, there are unique opportunities to test yourself against real challenges. Hiking, abseiling, rock climbing, yachting, surfing, windsurfing, canoeing, white water rafting, skiing: all require genuine courage.

To do these things without proper preparation is however no different to driving down the wrong side of the road at 140ks an hour. They are genuinely dangerous activities: all of them have killed many people over the years. Becoming an adult means having the sense to equip yourself mentally and physically with the right gear and the right learning.

Playing sport is still the most popular way for young Australians to test their strength, but it sometimes doesn't seem enough, judging by the number of successful young sports players who get in trouble for assaults and other self-destructive activities.

If you can't or don't want to take the options of sport or outdoor activities, how else can you test your courage in a world where there is little left to explore, where wars are – we hope – becoming less frequent, where young people are more and more supervised and controlled?

Some young men turn to second-hand adventures, playing computer games or fantasy games, reading fantasy books or going to adventure movies. The trouble is that these will never have the meaning of real experiences, and so ultimately are unsatisfying.

Testing courage is a relative thing, entirely. It is relative to your fears. If you have absolutely no fear of heights, parachuting or bungee-jumping might be fun for you, but probably won't have any other meaning. On the other hand if you're terrified of heights, diving off the high tower at the local pool is an achievement of great significance.

So the first thing to do to test your courage is to work out what your fears are. An American survey of people's fears came up with the surprising conclusion that speaking in public was people's greatest fear. If that's one of your fears, then go for it. The next time a teacher asks for a volunteer to give a sports report to the school assembly, put your hand up.

You may cause shock waves in the class, if you're not known for volunteering for stuff like that.

If you are picked, then give yourself every possible chance to succeed, by preparing your speech properly, and rehearsing it, preferably in the venue you're going to be using, and with the microphone on. That way you're less likely to be taken by surprise (and put off) if during your speech the microphone comes loose, or the lectern wobbles, or the air-conditioner blows your notes away. The audience may crack up, but if the speaker stays calm and dignified the audience quickly comes back to attention.

Your fears might include darkness, snakes, sex, being mocked, death, being fat, your father, your grandfather, being hurt, tests and exams, girls, dirt, failure, spiders . . .

You might be able to think of imaginative ways

you can find the courage to gradually (or quickly) overcome any of these fears. For example, if you have a fear of spiders, try becoming an expert on them. Do a science project on them, collect some spiders and put on a display in your school library or science lab.

If your fear is of girls, join a group where girls and boys mix in a friendly, easy way and relationships are not an issue.

If you're afraid of falling (which is a major reason some boys don't do well at sport) start a course in gym, where you'll be taught to roll and tumble on safe mats. That might give you the confidence to work up to throwing yourself around more. Tell the coach you're nervous, so he doesn't push you too hard, too fast. If he doesn't treat your fear with respect, change coaches.

Left uncontrolled, the mind can panic, which is not helpful to you at all. Panic is never helpful.

Here's a passage from one of my books, *The Dead of the Night*, where a character called Homer is speaking of courage:

> *'It's all in your head. You're not born with it, you don't learn it in school, you don't get it out of a book. It's a way of thinking, that's what it is. It's something you train your mind to do. I've just started to realise that. When something happens, something that could be*

> *dangerous, your mind can go crazy with fear. It starts galloping into wild territory, into the bush. It sees snakes and crocodiles and men with machine guns. That's your imagination. And your imagination's not doing you any favours when it pulls those stunts. What you have to do is to put a bridle on it, rein it in. It's a mind game. You've got to be strict with your own head. Being brave is a choice you make. You've got to say to yourself: "I'm going to think brave. I refuse to think fear or panic . . ."*
>
> *'Every time we panic, we weaken ourselves. Every time we think brave, we make ourselves stronger.'*

One of the topics I sometimes give students in my writing workshops is: *Think of your worst fear, then write a humorous piece about it*.

The point of this exercise, in writing terms, is that fear and comedy are closely related. One way we deal with our fears is by laughing at them. Take for example the common situation of a male being accidentally hit in the testicles (the balls) by a tennis ball. Spectators laugh long and loud at this sight and the commentators make jokes. Why? On the face of it there's no logical reason. A blow to the testicles is painful – sometimes extremely so – and sometimes very dangerous, causing permanent damage. The reason for the laughter then must surely be illogical, to do with the unconscious.

I suggest that it is because men have a strong unconscious fear of their penis or testicles being hurt, or worse, cut off. Freud explained this fear by saying that boys when very young notice that girls have no penis. They wonder if girls may once have had a penis, but lost it. They then fear that this might happen to them. Hence the jokes about castration, and the nervous laughter when someone's penis or testicles are hurt.

The writing exercise above is another way you can help yourself overcome your fears. Try it.

Not all our fears can be overcome simply by showing courage. Some can become phobias – extreme fears – like the fear of being fat, which in males and females can lead to eating disorders like anorexia. If you're suffering from a phobia, it is an extremely serious problem and you will need professional help – from a psychologist or someone similar.

One last thing: make sure you celebrate your achievements. If you have demonstrated your courage in a truly important and meaningful way, celebrate it. It is a wonderful thing you have done. Take pride in this great success. You are a stronger, more mature person as a result of it. Congratulations.

4. You Need To Earn Your Own Money

Money is one of the most powerful tools in our society. People often control other people through money. Parents often control their children through money, handing it out, withholding it, in a way which will give them a greater say in what their children do.

'You want money for a school excursion? OK.' 'You want money so you can go out with your friends? No way.'

That's not to say that parents shouldn't control their children. Of course they should. It's one of the important functions of parenting, and parents who don't realise that – and many don't – make life extremely difficult for their children.

But the control should lessen as the young person grows through adolescence, and the control should always be honest. The parent or parents should say openly: 'I don't want you to go out with your friends, for the following reasons . . .'

To engage in indirect control by giving or withholding money not only takes away the son's right to make his own decisions, but seems sneaky. It's using money as a weapon. If the parent can't convince the son that the parent's arguments are valid, then it could be that the son won't listen to reason, or it could be that the parent doesn't have a valid argument. Under the second circumstance the withholding of money would be wrong.

One of the least helpful things parents can do is to give their son large sums of money. If you have very wealthy parents they may leave all their money to you. What a terrible thing to do! You will go through life never knowing if you could have succeeded on your own. You have been cruelly blocked from realising your potential as a man.

Finding jobs where you can earn money while you're young, while you're still at school or a tertiary college, has never been easy. There are the old stand-bys like paper rounds, car-washing, baby-sitting, supermarkets. You can advertise in local shops and newspapers, or in a school newsletter. But as with most things in life, the more imaginative you are, the more successful you are likely to be. Businesses that do well are those which identify a need and come up with a creative solution. Figure out what your parents are most irritated by, most in need of. The chances are other people will have the same feelings and will pay someone who can ease them.

For example I'd happily pay someone who'd guarantee me same-day-service fixing minor computer glitches at a reasonable rate. Or someone who'd come round every three months and clean the leaves off my roof. Or someone who'd buy and deliver the regular groceries each week – the annoying stuff like milk and dog food and OJ that I have to pick up every time I go into a supermarket.

Is there something you can rent out maybe? It might be something you already own. Or something your parents own, and that you can do a deal with them over – a caravan, for instance. Or something you're prepared to buy and then rent to neighbours – a piece of computer equipment, or a shredder or mulcher or blower vac.

5. Learn Which Rules It's OK To Break

A survey of successful people, a few years ago, came up with a big surprise. The author of the survey expected to find that successful people came from similar backgrounds, or had similar educations, or shared similar philosophies.

Instead he found that they had only one thing in common. They all had what he described as a 'healthy disregard for the rules'.

In other words, they knew which rules to break, and when to break them.

One of the saddest sights I've ever seen was in Melbourne, about three o'clock one morning. A man stood at the corner of Flinders and Swanston Streets. He was waiting to cross. There were no cars in any direction. Not one. Yet the man waited until the little red figure on the traffic light turned to green.

He *waited until it turned to green!*

This is a human tragedy.

An immature person might react to all this by saying: 'Oh cool, he's telling us we can do whatever we want, break any rule we like.'

It's not that simple. Bob Dylan was once quoted as saying: 'If you're going to live outside the law, you gotta be honest.'

Laws are basically designed for the immature, but only a highly mature and moral (there's a tautology) person can ignore them. So, for example, the law says you're a murderer if you deliberately kill another human. But a doctor at a patient's deathbed, aware that the patient has only a couple of hours of agonised life left, might decide to give an injection which will end the patient's life.

Is the doctor wrong? I don't know. Certainly many religious people, and many philosophers, would say he or she is. Others would disagree. I do know that the doctor must be very sure of his or her ground, must be sure that he or she has thought the issues through in a most careful way, eliminating personal bias or neurotic influence. And I also know that such a doctor is no murderer.

A law says you mustn't steal. The law should be unnecessary, because we should be moral enough to know that stealing is wrong, but because many of us don't know that, the law is in place.

And there are even circumstances where you might decide stealing is a valid act – for example, if your child's life can only be saved by an expensive medicine that you can't afford. Or if you're starving to death, and your neighbour has an abundance of food.

One of the Spice Girls was quoted in October 1997 as saying, 'You can do anything you want, as long as you don't get caught.' If you believe in that approach, don't complain when a masked man smashes you in the face with a baseball bat, leaving you brain-damaged and blind. If the Spice Girl philosophy applies to you, then in fairness it has to apply to him too.

The Spice Girl morality is the morality of the three-year-old.

The truth is that you can do anything you want, as long as you accept the consequences. You can murder someone if you want – it's not difficult to find a weapon that'll kill someone – but among the consequences you'll have to accept are a lifelong torture of guilt and remorse, and probably many years in prison. You can cheat in a test, but the consequences might include having to live with your conscience, having to maintain that standard in future (you may have been promoted to a higher class as a result of your high mark), and the fact that you might have cut yourself off from getting the help with your work that you obviously need. If you are caught, there's the damage to your reputation, the loss of respect from others . . .

6. Find What You Believe In

Most young men in Australia today – and most adults – are in a very dangerous state. They have no spiritual belief.

That doesn't mean I'm trying to convert you to any particular religion. I'm not. Nevertheless people who have a strong religious belief may be better off than people who don't, in the short term anyway.

In the long term it can be unhealthy to commit to a religious system that you haven't thought through yourself. In other words it's better to come to a set of beliefs because you honestly, truly and deeply believe them, not because you've had them drummed into you all your life.

Among the major belief systems that have been practised in Australia are the aboriginal belief system, the Christian one, and more recently the Jewish and Islamic ones.

As well, smaller numbers of people are committed to Buddhism, Hinduism, Shinto, Baha'i and other religions.

The more you know about different religions, the better. The more you think about these issues, the better. At the end of your life you may not have come to any conclusion about God and religion, but at least you've given it your best shot. The dangerous state I spoke of, having no spiritual belief, applies only to people who don't think about this stuff, who don't even look for religious truth.

There is no more important topic for human beings to contemplate. Is there a God? Were we created or did we just happen? Is there a purpose to our existence? Is there a life after death? For as long as humans have existed we can be sure that they have wondered about these matters. There has never been, as far as we can tell, a society which has not believed in a god or gods.

Maybe the problems we have in western society are partly a result of our lack of belief. The fast growth of science has made us question everything, and trust only logical explanations. Science is dedicated to solving mysteries; religions are dedicated to maintaining them.

As well, many organised religions have done themselves damage by insisting on silly and meaningless doctrine, or have been damaged by their leaders' immoral activities.

Truth is truth, and if a religious leader steals money from his followers or sexually assaults some of them, it doesn't mean that the teachings of that religion are false. But it's not surprising that people feel angry, disillusioned and betrayed in those circumstances.

Karl Marx argued that 'religion is the opiate of the masses'; in other words, religion was cynically used by powerful people to keep the rest of the population under control. It was a drug that tranquillised them, so they didn't realise how awful their lives really were.

I don't know if that's true or not. I don't want to believe it, but even if there is some truth in it, I think the picture is more complicated than Marx suggested.

I suspect, though, that as religion has faded in importance for many people, they have found other things to replace it. One of the most obvious is sport. By becoming obsessed with sport, by following a team or a player with avid interest, by watching sport 'religiously' on TV, people escape from the reality of their lives.

'I reckon he deserves it', they say, generously, of a player being paid over a million dollars for losing the final of a tennis tournament. 'If you ask me they earn every cent', they say of a football team who get eight million dollars a season between them.

The speaker might be a panel beater with three children, who has worked for 15 years at his trade, who has the respect and admiration of his workmates and neighbours, and the love of his wife and children, who has nearly paid off half their suburban house . . . Yet he watches excitedly as a professional golfer lines up a putt in a skins tournament that could add another $100,000 to the golfer's $28 million fortune. And the panel-beater really cares! It really matters to him that the golfer sinks the putt!

Why? Is he on a 10 per cent commission?

I don't think so.

This man seems to underestimate his own value.

In 1996 I published a book called *This I Believe*. Before I plug it here I'd better point out that the profits from the book go to the Save the Children Fund, so I'm not promoting it now to make money for myself. But I recommend *This I Believe* to you. It contains over 100 short essays, most of them by famous Australians, in which each person states the beliefs he or she holds. They range from radical to conservative, from religious to atheistic, from narrow to wide.

By browsing through a book like this you may get a clearer focus on your own beliefs.

After you've done that, try writing such a statement yourself.

Incidentally, the fact that you believe in something doesn't mean you're locked in for life. There's no virtue in having a closed mind. You should always be open to new ideas, prepared to rethink your position. That's proof that you're alive. 'I think, therefore I am', said a famous French philosopher.

In a men's toilet in a restaurant in Fitzroy,

Melbourne, I saw this piece of graffiti: 'Opinions should be held as lightly as a leaf on a window sill: blown in any direction by the slightest puff of wind.'

Not your average graffiti. But I liked it, although it's worth noting that opinions and beliefs are two different things.

I suspect that one of the greatest enemies for human beings is cynicism. To be cynical is to believe in nothing, to think the worst of everyone, to be certain that everybody's trying to rip you off. There's no good in the world, everyone's just out for their own interests.

There is overwhelming evidence that the world's not like that, but cynical people don't want to know about it. Cynicism is like gastro: it goes through your whole system and makes you shitty.

You often get gastro because you haven't been clean yourself: you haven't washed your hands after going to the toilet. You get cynical because you haven't been trustworthy and honest and decent yourself. You think that because you're pretty grubby, the rest of the world must be equally grubby. It isn't.

The opposite to cynicism is trust.

7. Get Your Own Voice

When you speak, let us hear your thoughts, your opinions, your beliefs, your feelings. These are what make you unique as a human being, and they are what make you interesting to others.

And let it be in your words. Don't stand up in front of the whole school and say to a visitor: 'On behalf of the students of Mount Tomlin College I'd like to thank you for speaking at our Assembly this morning, and to say how honoured we are . . .'

Instead work out what you thought of the speech, and say that, remembering of course that certain courtesies apply.

> *Thanks for coming today. What you said about New Guinea made me realise that I didn't know anything about the place before this, which is pretty dumb considering it's our nearest neighbour. But now I wouldn't mind going there to check it out myself. So thanks for making us more aware of it.*

That's all you need.

Don't use the voice of a middle-aged person if you're not middle-aged:

> *I hope she fulfils all her expectations in her chosen field of study.*

This was part of a speech I heard in a country high school, when the school vice-captain was farewelling the captain, who was leaving for America.

When Queen Elizabeth II visited Parkes, NSW, a Year 11 student gave a welcoming speech:

> *Your visit will linger forever in our minds.*

Equally, when you write non-fiction – a history essay, for example, or a literature essay, or a letter – your voice should be heard clearly. Don't use words you wouldn't use in speech. Express yourself in words that are right for you. Don't write 'I purchased a bike' if you bought one. Don't write 'our accommodation was in a youth hostel' if you mean you stayed in one.

A Year 12 boy in Sydney, in his school magazine wrote:

> *. . . we must all make the little effort that is needed to keep our uniforms neat and tidy and behave in a manner that will surely give the school a reputation of fostering responsible, well-disciplined and courteous young members of society.*

That was written in 1993, not 1893. It sounds like a parent or teacher, not a 17-year-old.

It's not just teenagers either. Recently a New Zealand politician, being interviewed on national television, was asked if his government was going ahead with plans to shoot wild horses. He replied:

> *I think you can say there is a certain inevitability about that outcome.*

He meant 'Yes'. But he has become so strangled by language that he can't say the one simple word.

One of my first jobs was at the Water Board in Sydney. I was assigned to the Personnel Department and I spent three weeks going through job applications, removing original documents and shredding what was left. There were thousands of applications and it was a pretty boring job, so I started reading the letters as I shredded them. Before long their dullness and repetition began to grind away at my mind, like listening to someone singing the same song over and over:

> *Dear Mr Macdonald,*
> *I am writing to apply for the position advertised in the* Sydney Morning Herald *on April 15. My name is Marc Lennox and I am a Year 12 student at St Anne's High School. I am studying English, Economics, Physics, Biology and Indonesian. My interests are hockey, water-skiing, reading and music. The reason I think this job would suit me is because I have always liked . . .*

Yuck. No wonder Marc got an equally dull letter back thanking him for his application but informing him that the position had been filled by someone else.

If 80 people apply for the one position, and your letter is like 79 others in the pile, why should an employer hire you? Your letter has to be such that when the employer gets to the bottom of the pile, yours will be the one that sticks in his or her mind.

How can you achieve this? By the end of the three weeks at the Water Board there were a few letters that stuck in my mind. They were warm and personal; they were sincere, even passionate; they used humour; they struck a confident note; they engaged me as a reader.

I felt the personality of the writer in every line, and I liked their personalities. I wanted to meet those people and get to know them better.

That's personal voice.

John Kirkbride wrote a couple of quirky novels about job applications you might enjoy. The first is called *In Reply to Your Advertisement* and its sequel is called *Thank You for Your Application*.

When you speak or write for yourself, don't slip into false or imitative language. We've seen enough hypocritical language over the centuries. There's no need for you to add to it.

I collect examples of authentic personal voice.

Here's an example from football legend Ted Whitten, when his team, Victoria, had been beaten by South Australia:

> *I think it's important that we accept defeat gracefully, but speaking personally I'd have to say I'm a bit pissed off.*

When Australian cricketer David Boon was hit on the chest by a rising ball, Max Walker gave this vivid prediction of Boon's bruises:

> *He'll have a receipt for a couple of days, no doubt about that. The rings of Saturn will come out – green, purple, a sort of murky grey . . .*

I overheard this on a plane to Tasmania; from a passenger talking to the stewardess about his mate:

> *You can only take him anywhere twice, and the second time it's to apologise.*

Here's Terry Wheeler, ex-coach of the AFL Western Bulldogs team:

> *There are no trees on a football field, no rocks, nowhere to hide.*

I find that stark, direct and powerful.

And this is swimmer Tracey Wickham, talking about her disciplined approach to her sport:

> *There was one girl I used to swim against. She'd stand up there on the blocks beside me and I'd be 100 per cent serious and blocking everything out and here she'd be, this pretty blonde thing, winking at the boys and yapping away to me, saying things like, 'Gee, Tracey, I like your hair.' I like your hair! I'd think, No wonder you never do any good, your mind's all over the place. You're in the wrong place, kid. Go and do ballet or something.*

I'm not suggesting that Tracey's going to pick up any writing awards but there's something special about her language. And it's this: her voice comes through so powerfully. We know that we are hearing her self. It is authentic. As well, it's lively and engaging: a strong expression of her attitudes.

One highly important factor in voice is the influence of age. Teenagers have a different voice to children; middle-aged and old people are different again. A six-year-old won't come home from a birthday party and say to his mother: 'I scored the hottest chick in spin-the-bottle.' A school principal probably won't start an assembly with the words: 'Love ya, dudes! How's it all hanging?'

When young tycoon Lachlan Murdoch spoke at a press conference after a court victory for his Super League, he said: 'I was rapt . . .' Everyone laughed, so he quickly changed his words to 'Well, I was very happy.' He had been made to feel that his voice was wrong: too young for the situation in which he found himself.

What else affects voice? Gender, for sure. Men and women have always had different voices. 'Mate' was a male word in Australia for nearly 200 years, but women have been using it since about 1970. I still think of 'G'day, mate' as a male expression, but of course women use it. Words like 'sweet' and 'cute' have traditionally been female words, but it depends on the context: I can say 'This jam's too sweet', or 'This cake's too sweet', but I wouldn't feel comfortable saying 'You're a really sweet bloke.'

Personality and status are probably the biggest determinants of voice. You might remember the Anthony Browne book *Willie the Wimp*. Willie has the bad habit of apologising for everything. When he walks into a lamppost he apologises to the lamppost. He's low status and it shows. Low-status people tend to apologise all the time.

High status can be pompous ('It has come to my attention that some of your recent behaviour . . .')

or aggressive ('You can get stuffed, mate') or confident ('Put it there, thanks').

High-status people often use long words and long sentences. They do this because they are confident they won't be interrupted.

Your voice should be honest and confident, without being aggressive or overpowering.

8. Recognise Your Feelings

This is a big problem for a lot of males. Their failure to understand their feelings means they don't develop to their potential as human beings. In particular, they fail in relationships and they fail as fathers.

You certainly know men who are unable to confront or acknowledge their feelings.

A few years ago a Queensland politician said: 'In Queensland all males have their tear ducts surgically removed at birth.'

Sure, it's a funny line. But like most comedy, if you look at it from a different angle it's tragic. This guy has a big problem. When you deny your feelings, when you bottle them up, when you put them away, they don't disappear. They go deep inside you and they fester. It's like a dog burying a dead rabbit. It doesn't disappear. It sits there under the ground, getting rotten and mouldy.

As well as recognising your feelings you have to be able to express them, and express them in appropriate ways. If you're feeling angry it's not appropriate to hit someone. If you're frustrated it's not appropriate to destroy something. If you're depressed it's not appropriate to take drugs.

People who act like this aren't dealing with their feelings; they're either dumping them on someone else or trying to bury them.

It can take a lot of courage to confront and explore your feelings in a meaningful way.

The novel and film *Ordinary People* explore the life of a teenage boy who feels guilty about the death of his older brother in a boating accident. Conrad, who was a good swimmer, survived, but his brother drowned. As if that wasn't enough, Conrad is also struggling to cope with his parents, who are difficult people. Their relationship is in trouble, partly as a result of the drowning.

Conrad goes to a counsellor, who encourages him to express his feelings, not to bottle them up. One day he does so. Frustrated with his parents and grandparents during a family photo session he yells angrily at them.

They are shocked. He's never spoken to them like this before. They're very upset.

Conrad goes back to the counsellor. 'You told me to express my feelings,' he complains, 'and look what happened. They're all angry with me.'

The counsellor leans forward and says quietly: 'Don't expect it always to tickle.'

Conrad is a young man of great courage. At least one of his other friends, a girl he met in hospital, is unable to find as much courage. Rather than face up to her feelings she commits suicide.

Happiness, pride, love, they tickle. Anger, guilt, sorrow, they're a bit tougher to handle.

But how painful can feelings be, that people kill themselves rather than face them? How difficult is the truth? I keep thinking of a newspaper interview with an Anglican woman priest, who was trying to persuade some builders' labourers to go to church. One of them said: 'I'd rather stick a pin through my dick than go to church.' She thought: 'Goodness me, how painful can it be to go to church?'

Feelings can be extremely painful. But nothing's as painful as suicide. I'd rather go through the pain of confronting my feelings, no matter how much courage it takes, than throw my life away.

9. Experience Success

If you can't point to a number of major successes you've had in your life already, you need to do something about it.

This is quite urgent. There's nothing wrong with failing. Failures can be great. You can learn heaps from them, you can become stronger, you can bounce back next time.

To fail time and time again, however, is a very

different matter. It is a serious problem that needs to be addressed. It is very bad for you to fail over and over. There is nothing to be gained from it.

I once took over as coach of a tennis team that had been losing every game by big margins for years. I said to the man who appointed me: 'If after one year of hard work the team are still the easybeats of the competition, I will come to you and tell you that we must withdraw. We must find different teams to play against, teams who are closer to our level.'

As it happened the team did improve steadily, and although they did not win a match that season they were no longer easybeats. And they won their first match of the following season.

That's irrelevant though; the point I want to make is that the choices for a person or a team in their situation were very easy. Improve or get out.

If you are failing badly in a music course, a relationship, the job market, a sport, a school subject, school generally, then that is your choice: improve or get out. It is dangerously easy to drift along for month after month, year after year. It's often more comfortable to do that, to stay in your unhappy hole, than to risk breaking new ground. It takes energy to break new ground, and people who have been failing for a long time lose energy.

A battery that keeps being drained becomes flat. It needs to be recharged. If you're feeling like that battery, drained by failure after failure, never getting the recharge of a success, you need to take charge of the situation.

Supposing we're talking about a school subject for instance. If you've been failing in Maths or Japanese for months or years, you're doing yourself damage. Work out a programme for the next four weeks that you think you can manage. It might involve getting help from your parents, another student, a teacher, a computer programme or a different book. Don't aim to reach an A or make up all the ground you've lost. Just give yourself targets you can attain.

If after four weeks you haven't made any progress it might be that this subject just isn't your scene. Your skills may lie elsewhere. Quit.

But it's not enough to put an end to a long run of failures. You've got to achieve some success. Real success too: you on your own, without cheating, without having your hand held. Choose something that you're really keen to do, work out how you're going to do it, discipline yourself to achieve it.

Avoid that very common mistake of taking on too much.

You might decide that you're going to achieve success by getting a job, by putting out a class yearbook, by designing and selling a range of T-shirts, by getting your coaching certificate in soccer or your umpire's accreditation in cricket, by reaching Grade Six in saxophone, by making a movie, by saving enough money for something you want, by building a sleep-out, by swimming a sub-minute 100 metre freestyle, by quitting smoking, by taking over the cooking for your family at weekends, by reading a book a fortnight for the next year . . .

'Nothing succeeds like success' says the old proverb. Success is good for humans and other living creatures!

10. Explore Your Feelings About Death

A person who has no understanding of death, never grappled with it, never thought about it, is not yet an adult.

A generation or two ago children saw life at close quarters. In some societies they still do – but not in our urbanised, industrialised, contemporary Australia. Beatrix Potter, author of *Peter Rabbit*, in a letter to a newspaper in 1911 described how as a child she had helped scrape the bristles off her grandmother's slaughtered pig. She complained, 'The present generation is being reared upon tea – and slops.'

Maxim Gorky, in his classic account of pre-Revolutionary Russia, *My Childhood*, wrote with vivid detail of his first-hand encounters with suffering, depravity, happiness, life – and death:

> *Nanny took his cap off, and the back of his head hit the floor with a dull thud. Then it rolled over to one side, and the blood flowed more abundantly, but only from one corner of his mouth now. It flowed for a horribly long time. At first I expected Tsiganok to rest a little, sit up, spit something out and say:*
>
> *'Whew! It's hot in here!'*
>
> *He always used to say this on Sundays, when he woke up from his after-supper nap. Now he didn't get up, but he just lay there, his life ebbing away.*
>
> *The sun had already moved away from him and the bright strips of light had shortened and fell on the window sills. Tsiganok had gone black all over, his fingers didn't move any more, and the foam had dried from his lips. Around his head burnt three candles, their flickering golden spears lighting up his dishevelled, blue-black hair, his blood-stained teeth and the tip of his sharp nose, throwing quivering yellow patches on his swarthy cheeks.*
>
> *Nanna, who was kneeling by him and weeping, whispered: 'My angel, light of my life.'*
>
> *It was cold in the room and I hid under the table in terror. Then my Grandfather, in his*

raccoon-fur coat, burst into the kitchen, followed by Grandmother, who was wearing her cloak with the little tails hanging on the corridor, Uncle Mikhail, and a lot of strangers.

Grandfather flung his coat on the floor and roared 'Bastards! Feel satisfied now you've killed him? He would have been worth his weight in gold in five years' time!'

(pp. 58–59)

In our antiseptic, terrified society, where avoiding the experience of death for ourselves and for others has become a national obsession, will we ever again find anyone who can write with such intimate, loving knowledge of the mysteries of human existence?

I once taught a class of Year 10 students. We were reading a book called *Bless the Beasts and Children* in which the young characters suddenly come across buffalo being slaughtered. My Year 10 students yawned their way through this chapter of the book, showing no interest in the scene, no understanding of the feelings involved.

I thought 'Stuff this, I'll show them what it's like to unexpectedly come across animals being killed.'

I drove to the local abattoir and got permission to bring my class there the next day. When the students arrived at the classroom I loaded them in a bus and we drove straight to the abattoir. Not until we were at the gates did the students realise where we were going.

The trip had a dramatic effect on them. Only three were able to complete the tour; the rest ended up sitting outside under trees with their heads on their knees, trying to quell their nausea. Four became vegetarians on the spot.

For many years these students had happily helped buy meat in neat Gladwrapped packets in the supermarket. They had happily helped cook it, and they had happily eaten it. Now, for the first time, they were confronted with the reality of where the meat had come from. They understood in a real (not an abstract) way that the animals had to be killed before they could be eaten, and they started to understand what those deaths involved.

It's morbid to be obsessed with death. But it's equally unhealthy to avoid thinking about it. As part of your Science or Religion or English course you might be able to do a unit on death. This could involve a visit to an undertaking business or a crematorium, discussion with a doctor, a visit to an abattoir.

11. Don't Have Heroes

When you 'worship' a hero, you're saying that he's better than you. And as if that's not bad enough, you might even be saying that he's perfect.

Right away there's two good reasons you shouldn't have heroes.

People who 'worship' others have something lacking in themselves, something missing in their own make-up. They lack confidence. The truth is that everyone in the world, including you, is a complex mixture of good and bad, strength and weakness. You may steal something from a shop one minute, but the next minute you sponsor your mate in the 40 Hour Famine, for more than you can really afford. You may be excellent at Art but hopeless at Maths, brilliant at writing lyrics for a band at school but a disaster at football.

Do you really imagine your hero is any different? He might be a genius at football but hopeless with relationships; he might be a guitar legend who selfishly hogs the limelight; he might be a top actor but a chronic liar as well.

Inevitably one day you'll read a newspaper article showing that your hero is actually a violent psychopath despised by all who know him, or a show-off, or a cheat.

What is OK is to respect good qualities and good deeds by other people. So I admire the courage of Pastor Kolbe, who in World War II took the place of an innocent man condemned to death by the Germans; I like the music of Bob Marley; I respect the art of Brett Whiteley; I'm impressed by the cricketing skills of Sir Donald

Bradman. At the same time I'm aware that Marley and Whiteley were wrecked by drugs, and some of Bradman's team-mates considered him a selfish player.

It's equally immature to make heroes out of people you know. Fathers, uncles, brothers, students at your school: for all their fine qualities they still don't qualify as heroes. Be satisfied with enjoying their company and appreciating their achievements. Recognise that you have many fine qualities yourself. There are lots of people who enjoy and appreciate what you have to offer.

If that's not the case, if you are unpopular, then there are reasons for that. It would be more helpful to look at those reasons than to spend your time admiring the false images you have constructed in your mind of other people. I'll come back to that later in this book.

12. Give

Giving is one of the greatest pleasures of being an adult.

Sure, a kid can give, but his opportunities are severely limited. He mightn't have the skills to make anything too dazzling, he probably doesn't have the strength to do a lot of stuff for others, he usually doesn't have much money for presents, and often when he does he knows the money isn't really 'his', it came from his parents.

An adult has the skills and strength; he's also more likely to have the time and money.

My first real experience of giving came when I was about 17. During school holidays I occasionally went on Meals-on-Wheels, helping to deliver meals to old people who were in their homes but unable to take proper care of themselves. For many of these people the Meals-on-Wheels volunteers were the only visitors they saw. They welcomed the food, but even more, they valued the social chat.

For me it was a chance to see a different world, a world I hadn't known existed. I was interested in the stories the old people told of their lives. I felt good about the value they placed on our visits.

Since then there have been periods of my life where I've done quite a lot for others and periods where I haven't done nearly enough. Particularly satisfying, though, have been the times when I've worked in the so-called 'helping professions'. The time I spent in hospitals, and the time I spent teaching, were easily the most satisfying jobs I've had.

You can give your time, to volunteer work. You can give your money. An old Christian tradition is 'tithing': the idea that you give 10 per cent of your income away. I remember reading a bit of advice somewhere, that you should give 10 per cent, save 10 per cent, and spend the rest.

You can give presents. These don't have to be

bought in shops. You can give someone a poem you've written or copied out for them, maybe on an unusual surface, like bark or a shoe or paper you've made. You can give jewellery you've created out of a beautiful stone you found in a river, or at the beach. You can give flowers or a pot plant that you've grown from seed. Make a tape of their favourite songs. Record a piece of music that you play yourself; better still, one that you've composed yourself.

Another great gift is a promise: to mow the lawn for a year or write a letter to the person every fortnight, or clean the windows every month.

As with most things in life, being creative is a definite bonus.

These presents will be highly valued, and you'll feel pretty damn pleased when you see the pleasure your gifts have brought.

There's a lot to becoming a man. It's a huge challenge. Even huger if you don't know any men who are mature. If there's no men close to you who are setting a strong example you'll have to do it on your own. But that's OK. It's been done by others and it can be done again. By you.

Just to make it harder though, there are even more points that I haven't covered here, because they're kind of obvious. Things like:

Being self-disciplined
Respecting the rights of others
Working hard
Staying fit

The good news is that you can do it. You have it within you to become a man in the true sense of the word. Remember, it's not a race. You can spend a few years on it. At the end of the journey you can take your place in your community, as an adult to be respected, a person to whom others will come for advice, a leader.

TRUTH AND LIES

Telling lies has become part of our society. We may be the first culture in the history of the world where many of our leaders regularly tell lies and get away with it. Not just political leaders but sporting leaders, business leaders, even religious leaders.

And not good lies either, if there are such things (which is doubtful). Lies designed to cover their wrongdoing, lies to help them gain power and money, lies which show their contempt for those who have respected and admired them.

We've been a concealing culture for a long time. It hasn't worked. By concealing child abuse, domestic violence, corporate fraud, our society has made the damage from these acts worse.

'The (whaling) industry has a history of deceit . . .' said an ABC television reporter recently, during a story on the slaughter of protected species of whales by Japan. The result of this lying has been the almost complete destruction of many species of whales.

When tennis player Patrick Rafter admitted that he was drunk during the 'dead rubber', the last match in a Davis Cup tie which Australia had already won, a lot of people were outraged. Former champion Ken Rosewall commented: 'I think it's been done before by players in that situation but I think it hasn't generally been acknowledged . . . it's been kept private . . .'

In other words, in previous times hypocrisy ruled: privately people did one thing, publicly they pretended something else. Rafter's main crime wasn't being drunk; it was being honest.

'Telling lies to the young is wrong' is the title of a famous poem by Russian poet Yevgeny Yevtushenko. In fact telling lies to anyone is wrong. Adults don't have the right to lie to you, even if it's 'for your own good'. No-one has the right to decide on behalf of someone else what they should or shouldn't be allowed to know.

Your right to the truth takes precedence over adults' right to keep you in ignorance.

Melbourne newspaper *The Age* recently carried this report:

> *. . . Those naughty giant snuff puppets have been told to cover up or keep off the boardwalk. Just before they were about to strut their*

festival stuff, the snuff puppeteers were informed that they had to cover up the private parts protruding from their puppets. (Naked puppets as tall as five metres leave little to the imagination.) They were also told to excise some of the mock violence from their routines.

A spokesman for the snuff puppets, Andy Freer, says they have been performing their routine in the City Square without any modifications. He says their act is black comedy intended to challenge notions of violence in society. 'Each time we are asked to cover up and soften the act, it's always on the pretext that we upset the kids,' says Freer. 'The kids love us. It's their parents who keep dragging them away.'

One of the most popular lies aimed at children is that there is a Santa Claus. And a tooth fairy and an Easter Bunny. Parents know perfectly well that there is no Santa, but they lie to their children about it. They do so because they claim it's sweet and cute and children love it. The truth is, it's adults who need Santa. Children make up their own stories and fantasies and games. They don't need extra ones invented by adults.

Adults need Santa because they desperately want to believe that there's still innocence and goodness in the world. Of course there is, but many adults are scared there mightn't be. Rather than look at their fears honestly they hide within the comforting arms of Santa. Unfortunately there is no comfort in lies, and these people often end up more confused than ever.

In 1996 an English newspaper quoted an eight-year-old girl who'd been asked her opinion on Santa. 'I believe in him,' she said, 'because my Mummy wants me to.'

For many young people, finding out that there is no Santa is no big deal. For others it is traumatic. They see it as a betrayal by their parents. They are shocked to find that their parents have lied to them for all these years.

But the Santa lie is far from being the only lie perpetrated in Australia in recent times. Among the lies specifically aimed at adolescents are these:

1. By going to school you'll make something of yourself (and get a job)

Going to school can be important, but it's really to do with socialisation and economics. Schools teach you the 'rules' for society, many of which are questionable anyway. For example they teach you to sit quietly in large groups and obey the orders of adults. They teach you how to play sport in large groups. They teach you to work in a room with a lot of other people. They teach you how to take part in a discussion with a lot of other people.

These skills can be useful, but another reason for teaching them is so you will learn to fit in with society, you won't rock the boat. Today you learn how to sit quietly in class, tomorrow you'll have a 9 to 5 job, a house with a mortgage, and 2.3 kids.

Melbourne principal David Loader has written of our school system: 'Does such an experience create an educative environment for our young people? Does it lull them into sleep or complacency, leaving leadership and responsibility to others? Is this how the victim mentality begins? Does it encourage students to take responsibility for their own lives? Worse, does it create anger and annoyance which expresses itself in a passive aggression? In some students it creates overt anger . . .' (*The Inner Principal*, Falmer Press)

On the other hand maybe society needs this kind of education system if it is to survive. We keep students in schools because we see it as important to socialise them, so that they don't destroy the culture that has been constructed over a number of generations. If you think our society is basically a good one, then you may think schools are a good way to keep it strong.

Most of the other stuff you learn in school would be best taught in other ways. Australian schools are not good models for learning environments. If parents wanted children to learn as much as possible they wouldn't put them in a western-style school.

You could take a year off school, for example to travel around Australia with your parents, and it would make almost no difference to your school progress. You'll learn far more than your peers who spent the year in the classroom.

We also keep young people in schools because it's a relatively cheap and efficient way of looking after them while their parents are at work, or busy in other ways. We don't trust them to be on their own. We trust adults to be on their own, but not teenagers. It might be better if adults were to teach young people how to look after themselves, so that they didn't have to be supervised all the time.

One way we succeed in keeping adolescents in schools is by putting great pressure on them. They are given the strong impression that their whole life will be blighted if they drop out of education.

This is cruel and unfair, as well as untrue. If you decide to leave school before Year 12, there are plenty of different ways you can continue your education as an adult, should you decide that's the way you want to go.

2. Adults can be trusted

This unfortunate lie has caused terrible grief for many people over the years. Some adults can be trusted, some can't. The fact is that some adults are abusive, dishonest, violent, just as others are honest, decent, sincere.

Equally, of course, some young people can be trusted, and some can't.

You will know some adults who believe that they should be trusted and respected automatically, because they've been alive for a certain number of years; because they've had a certain number of birthdays.

Unable to earn respect in any other way they have to rely on their age to get it for them.

Chronological age is irrelevant. What matters are people's emotional age, their spiritual age, their mental age, their social age. I have known people of 12 who are well-balanced, intelligent, thoughtful, empathetic. I have known people of 60 who are spiteful, selfish, prejudiced, shallow.

Who can we trust? The answer is, the truly mature person, and that person could be 12 or could be 60.

On the other hand if you believe no adults can be trusted you have a serious problem. The cause for this belief will undoubtedly lie in your early life experiences, but it's up to you to set to work now to unlearn this attitude. Otherwise it will keep adding to your grief.

3. Your parents know what's best for you

In a culture which treats parents as gods it's very hard for teenagers of destructive, negligent or immoral parents. There's a lot of pressure on the sons of such parents to believe that if they are angry or rebellious they must be bad sons.

Some destructive parents are very good at presenting an image to the outside world of being loving and caring. In this situation it can be difficult for the son to trust his own feelings: he thinks his anger and depression, his frustration and confusion must be his fault. His parents have convinced him, just as they have convinced others.

If you're interested in reading more about this subject try reading Alice Miller's *The Drama of the Gifted Child*, also known as *The Drama Of Being a Child*.

Luckily most parents try to do the right thing for their children. When they make mistakes the damage is reduced by the fact that they have done so many good and loving things for their sons. Everyone, including your mother and father, is entitled to make bad calls. It's fair enough that sometimes they're unjust, selfish, lazy, bad-tempered. In well-functioning families everyone gets over it sooner or later.

In families with problems those things happen too often, or, even worse, they're not balanced by lots of good moments: times when parents are loving, good-humoured, understanding, generous.

There's an old saying that first you love your parents, then you hate them, then you forgive them.

There can be some truth in that. No matter how much you might hate your parents at some stage of your life (and that stage might be now) you still feel some love for them. If you really hate them at the moment you might furiously deny that; you mightn't want to believe it; but it is true nonetheless.

The quicker you can move through that to forgiveness, the better for you. It'll make your life easier. Only when you've made your peace with them are you free from the distraction of hating them. Hating is just about a full-time business. Until you forgive your parents you'll put so much energy into hating them that you'll hardly be able to live your own life.

4. Hard work brings rewards

How simple life would be if this were true. All the hard-working people would end up rich and all the lazy people would end up poor. All the hard-working athletes would end up with gold medals and all the slack ones would come last. Justice would be done.

A moment's thought should show you how silly this belief is. In real life someone who works hard for 50 years might have their uninsured house destroyed by a fire and be left with nothing. An old-age pensioner has his life savings stolen by a con-man or a burglar.

A slob wins six million dollars in the lottery. A

rich man gives his son a BMW convertible for his eighteenth birthday. Rupert Murdoch and Kerry Packer promote their sons to powerful and important positions in their organisations by the time they're 25, positions they could not hope to achieve for another 10 or 15 years if they had a different surname, or more likely, positions they could never hope to achieve.

The truth is that hard work is more likely than laziness to bring success. There are no guarantees though. Other factors, like luck, play a part. But it's good for the soul to work hard. There's a sense of satisfaction, a feeling of achievement, when you give it your best, over a long period of time. You can't hope to reach full adulthood, to be a man in the best sense of the word, unless you're prepared to get your hands dirty.

5. There's something wrong with you if you don't read

Many boys prefer not to read. They have other things they'd rather do. Yet great pressure is put on them by adults who feel, sometimes with desperate urgency, that these boys must read. The boys are made to feel that there is something wrong with them because they choose not to read.

It's true that life is more difficult if you don't have good reading skills. It's harder for you in the workplace, it's harder in social situations. You need to be able to read so that you can follow maps in street directories, understand manuals for equipment you've bought, read reports that might be important in business, read the computer screen. But as long as you have those skills, it's fine if you choose not to make reading one of your hobbies.

You may prefer to go water-skiing, play computer games, make kites, watch movies. These can all be worthwhile activities, and may be better than reading, if the only reading you do is of junk.

The main reasons for reading in your spare time are that it can give great enjoyment, it helps your reading skills, and it's also a powerful source of information and ideas.

6. Your dreams will come true if you believe in them enough

OK, right now I'm dreaming I'll be the next Olympic high jump champion . . . I'm sitting here dreaming it, waiting for it to happen . . . come on, why isn't it happening? Oh come on, what's the problem here? COME ON, HURRY UP, I WANT THAT GOLD MEDAL AND I WANT IT NOW!

Doesn't work, does it?

This 'you can do anything you want as long as you believe in yourself' rubbish is a shallow cheap-fix attempt to solve a serious problem, that of lack of confidence and self-esteem.

It is true though that a lot of people don't set their sights high enough.

I remember reading an article in a magazine years ago about a man named John Goddard, who had set 100 major goals he wanted to achieve in his life. At the time the article was written he had achieved 81 of his targets. They included things like flying a jet faster than the speed of sound, skippering a submarine, and travelling down the River Nile in a canoe.

It's a bit excessive to set that many difficult goals because your interests will probably change as time goes on, and you mightn't want to lock yourself in for too long. But there could be a lot of value in setting yourself 10 or 15 or 20 hard-to-achieve goals. Competing in a triathlon. Being accepted for the Big Brother programme. Getting your motorbike licence. Doing a grade 20 rock climb. Visiting Uluru. Getting your first poem or short story published. Running a marathon . . .

Make sure there's balance in your goals. Don't let all of them be sports-oriented, for example.

MORE LIES

Among the lies adults tell themselves about adolescents to justify their treatment of them:

1. Young people are impressionable

This is the biggest lie in some ways, as it underpins all adult attitudes to the young.

Being impressionable doesn't automatically go with age. You find impressionable people of all ages, including the old and the middle-aged and the young. You find strong-minded people of all ages, including the old and the middle-aged and the young. If you've ever tried to persuade a three-year-old to eat spinach you'll soon see how impressionable they are. If you've ever tried to persuade someone to switch their support of one football team to another, or to stay at a party they really want to leave, or to read a book they don't want to read, you'll find how impressionable they are.

Someone told me how in a bank one day they saw a mother trying to make her little son sit, so she could go to the teller. After a long struggle she finally got him to sit. As she walked away, the kid muttered: 'I might be sitting on the outside, but I'm still standing on the inside.'

That's a strong spirit: the statement shows what a feisty little guy he is. Hardly weak or soft or impressionable.

The history of Nazi Germany shows that Hitler had no trouble finding disciples among the old and the middle-aged. He found millions upon millions of them, enough to run a worldwide war for six years.

When we look at the sect run by the Reverend Jim Jones, in Georgetown, Guyana, a sect which ceased to exist when Jones persuaded all his followers to commit suicide, we see the success of yet another fraudulent guru in persuading the old and the middle-aged to give their lives (literally) to him.

There are quite a few young drug addicts, sure, but there are quite a few old ones too. The oldest person to die from heroin addiction in Victoria in 1997 was a 70-year-old woman in Wangaratta.

There are an awful lot of middle-aged and old alcoholics.

What is true is that first experiences make a strong impression on people. And what is also true is that you have more first experiences in childhood and adolescence. The first time you control your bladder and bowels, the first time you get in trouble, the first time you have sexual feelings, the first time you see a dead person, drive a car, travel overseas, make love, get dropped by a girlfriend or boyfriend . . . all these things are extremely powerful. They are so powerful that the way you regard this activity will probably be affected for a long time – perhaps forever – by the way you experienced it that first time.

For example, if the first time you play with your penis you get a smack, just when the feelings are getting really exciting, you may become nervous about anything later which involves your penis. If your first plane trip is a nightmare, with the plane bouncing around in a storm and people screaming, you mightn't be too keen on flying again.

If it's your hundredth flight it mightn't bother you too much. (On the other hand if the plane loses all power and drops 10,000 feet before the engines restart, you might never want to fly again, even if you're an experienced traveller. So this rule about first-time experiences isn't the whole story.)

The person buying their eleventh car isn't likely to be wildly excited, unless it's their first sports car perhaps. An undertaker yawns as another body comes in. If you live in Sydney you probably hardly notice the Harbour Bridge any more.

Yes, we can say that first experiences are nearly always very powerful, very important. *They make a strong impression*. Hence the belief that adolescents are impressionable. All those first experiences can push you in different directions – even directions that surprise you.

This still doesn't explain why some people are easily led, talked into acting in horrifying ways, like the disciples of Hitler, Jones, Manson, Pol Pot.

We find the explanation for their behaviour in their childhood. They are usually people who have been dominated by their parents. They often have strict fathers (often abusive), and mothers who only gave them love if they behaved a certain way. Unable to grow up, completely immature, easily dominated by people who act the same way their parents did, they are easy targets for power-maniacs. They are a strong example of why growing up is such a good idea.

2. Young people are illiterate, rude, drug addicted, loud uncaring louts who swear, spit, have no respect for adults, and won't do what they're told

These beliefs about the young come from a few causes. Certainly there's often something a bit lawless about adolescents. Some of them challenge the rules, break the law, defy authority. Some go further and tear the rule book up completely.

A lot of adults are nervous of adolescents. A lot are angry at them. A lot are jealous of them. Sometimes adolescents seem to have a freedom – including a sexual freedom – that adults envy.

It can happen that an adult who's trapped in a boring, joyless life will resent a group of young people on the train who are making a lot of noise and seem to be having a good fun-filled time.

Here's an item from *The Age*:

The tram, route number 1, was trundling along in the late afternoon, bearing from South Melbourne to the city its usual collection of late shoppers, shift workers and school kids. The students, 12- to 14-years-olds, were showing all the normal signs of being grateful for their deliverance from purgatory. They hoo-hooed a bit, kicked their bags around, spoke in loud voices, told silly jokes, and generally enjoyed themselves.

Fellow passengers took it in their stride, but not the conductor. It was too much, he said. These rabble-rousers would have to leave the conveyance and walk the rest of the way into Melbourne. Begone, said he. So, as the tram pulled into the Arts Centre corner, the youngsters stood up, formed a line and slowly trooped off.

As they did, they sang, in lovely two-part harmony, 'You've lost that Loving Feeling,' (Righteous Brothers, we seem to recall). The biggest kid, who appeared to be the leader, paused on the step, turned back to the conductor, and moaned back the chorus at him: 'Whow-whow-whow!' The performance was choreographed to the second; the sound was superb.

And the remaining passengers clapped them off.

Some adults feel they should be respected just because they are adults, and when they don't get that automatic respect they are angry.

Here's the opening few paragraphs in a story written by an adult in 1997. Her view of teenagers is conveyed without much subtlety:

Mrs Fosters toiled up the steps of the bus, steeper with every painful trip.

'Move it, you stupid old bat.'

'Useless old witch.'

Shocked expressions rippled over the faces of the older passengers. The bus driver scowled into the rear-vision mirror.

'Quiet down the back,' he yelled.

'He's got the hots for the old bag,' jeered a girl, angelic round face under a gleaming cap of gold curls.

'Olds should be put down,' said Miss Purple-streaked hair, in a loud voice.

'We'll end up being late because of the stupid old hag,' announced sweet faced 12-year-old.

It seems that some adults can't imagine that many or most teenagers actually behave in a decent civilised way most of the time.

The truth is that some young people do act rudely. The truth is, so do some adults.

The manners of teachers, for example, are often appalling. Recently I was at a country high school which had a sign outside the staffroom door:

THESE WORDS WILL HELP YOU GET A GOOD RESPONSE TO YOUR REQUEST:

Excuse me.
Please.
Thank you.
Would it be convenient.
May I.

That's fine, but the problem is that teachers don't use these words themselves when dealing with students. They don't treat students with courtesy and respect.

Of the thousands of schools I've visited, only eight have allowed students into the staffroom. At these schools, teachers who wished to speak to students invited them in, offered them a cup of coffee, and student and teacher sat in armchairs to have their chat.

These schools were without exception great schools. Not because they allowed students into the staffroom, but because they treated students politely and with respect. The way teachers sat in the armchairs and chatted with them was just one symptom of that.

On the other hand I went to a school recently where a teacher began every lesson by marching into the classroom yelling, 'Places, feet, mouths.'

He meant: 'Go to your places, stand on your feet, and close your mouths.'

How offensive! Would he have spoken that way to a class of adults?

At another school I arrived in the library to give a speech to Year 10 students, and found they had been told to sit on the floor for my 50 minute talk. As I walked in a student arriving at the same time realised what he was in for. 'I'm not sitting on the fucking floor', he said furiously.

I didn't blame him. Adults arriving in the library to listen to a 50-minute speech would never, never, never be asked to sit on the floor. The lack of any seating arrangements was an insult to the young people in this class.

At the same school, when I finished my speech – chairs having been found for the students – the librarian addressed the audience: 'Gentlemen,' she began, then added sarcastically, 'if I can call you that . . .'

Would she have spoken to adults like that? Does she imagine adolescents are impervious to such insults?

After thanking me for coming to the school she turned to another teacher and noted that we'd finished early. 'Recess doesn't start for five minutes', she said, and then, in the hearing of the students: 'Do you think we can trust them out there for five minutes on their own?'

She seemed like a nice lady. I'm sure she was. I'm sure she didn't strangle cats or sell heroin to

Grade Two kids or steal walking frames from old people in nursing homes. So when she's faced by a group of adolescents why does she feel it's OK to be so gratuitously rude?

> *'It's awful being a kid; no-one listens to you.' Lisa Simpson*
>
> *'It's rotten being old; no-one listens to you.' Homer's father*
>
> *'It's great being a white male, age 18 to 49, they listen to everything you say.' Homer Simpson*

At another school the teacher complained bitterly that the Year 11 students were passive. I found them passive too. They sat apathetically gazing at me as I spoke, then did some writing exercises, but they didn't seem very involved. I noticed that while this was going on the teacher, seated near me, was preparing her next lesson, going through a copy of *Romeo and Juliet* and making notes. She apparently didn't feel there was anything rude about her doing that while the students and I worked to improve our writing skills.

At the end of the session she gave a little speech about pushing the chairs into the tables, and watched closely as students did what she asked. Anyone who didn't push the chairs in was called back to do it properly. I understood why the students were passive.

The other day at a school in Sydney the principal introduced me to the students with a flowery address about my life and career. He spoke for quite a long time, then I stood to start my speech. I was surprised to see the principal's back as he disappeared through the exit door. The way he'd spoken, I'd thought he'd be in the front row taking notes. It seemed rude to me, that he would introduce me but not bother to listen to what I had to say. Obviously I just didn't rate highly enough with him. If I'd been the Prime Minister he would have stayed.

I can't say I've noticed a lot of terrible behaviour in this generation of young people. Like most people they tend to react the way they're treated. However they have thrown away many of the old rules of etiquette, good manners. This is quite reasonable, as society has changed, and many of those old rules were stupid anyway.

For instance, I was taught that if you go to someone's house for dinner, you should always leave a little bit of food on the side of your plate, to show that you'd had enough. Otherwise the people who cooked the dinner might think you're still hungry: they should have given you more food. But nowadays I think most guests would say 'Great dinner. Any of those shasliks left?'

3. Young people don't speak properly

The complaint is that 'in my day' people spoke 'properly' and now they mispronounce words or give new meaning to old words.

This needs to be translated. What they mean is that 'The English language should be frozen in time at the year 1950', or whenever they were growing up.

There's just a hint of vanity here. These people are saying that they are so important that the whole evolution of English should be halted at the point when they learned it.

It never occurs to them that Shakespeare or Milton or the translators of the Bible – names they often mention as speakers of 'good' English – would be appalled if they heard these people talking. No doubt these great poets would say: 'Call that English? That's not English! Now in my day . . .'

A language that stops growing and changing is a dead language.

4. Girls are bitchy, boys are more direct

The theory is that girls are gossipy, into backstabbing, really vicious. When they have an argument with someone it goes on forever. Boys on the other hand are more open. If they're mad at each other they have a fist fight and get it over and done with. Then they shake hands and everyone lives happily ever after.

It's amazing how many people devoutly believe this pretty picture and how long this myth has lasted.

It's not true. So many guys love to gossip, and so much male conversation is gossip. You don't believe me? Try listening to your father and his mates next time they're around the barbie. Try listening to your mates next time they're talking at the bus stop.

Most boys and men avoid fist fights most of the time.

As so often though we're in generalisation city here. There are plenty of exceptions among both genders.

I think it is true though that men and women often use different weapons. The female weapon is often words, the male weapon often fists or other physical tactics. In recent years there has been a huge campaign against men using violence. Fair enough too. But to go side by side with that campaign we need another one, against the damage done by women's verbal and emotional abuse. It's not a question of which is worse. Both forms of abuse – fists and words – are dangerous and damaging and destructive.

At the same time as we get those campaigns up and running, we should start another one, to end physical violence by women, and another one, to end verbal violence by men. Cover all the bases.

Men and women need to learn to solve problems without trying to carve pieces off each other. They need to learn to handle their rage. They need to concentrate on solutions not problems.

Most issues aren't really gender issues at all. They're human issues.

ADULTS AND TEENAGERS

For a while the generation gap was the size of the Grand Canyon. My parents listened to Bing Crosby and Fred Astaire, women stayed at home and ironed the sheets and pillowcases, men kept one job all their lives. My father worked for the Commonwealth Bank for 48 years.

But the kids my age listened to the Beatles and the Rolling Stones, wore jeans, got into drugs, were serious about being creative and achieving individual freedom.

This is a massive generalisation, but it was true for many people. Most of it was true for me, except that the only drugs I've taken are Panadol, Diet Coke and the occasional bottle of wine.

Nowadays parents and their children tend to

like the same music, talk the same language, get involved in each other's lives.

Let's not get too carried away though. The fact is that there's still a big generation gap.

Some of the biggest differences are over subjects like money, drugs, schoolwork, sex and relationships with girls, curfews, household jobs, friends who your parents don't like.

Adults have set up a tough world for teenagers and are often the first to complain that the teenagers aren't grateful. In fact they can be furious when anyone points out how difficult that world is.

There are in fact not many ways in which today's teenagers have it better than their parents or grandparents. Certainly they own more stuff than any other generation of young people in the history of the world. But that's not necessarily a good thing.

Many of them do get more care and attention from their parents, though that's not necessarily a good thing either. It's all a question of balance. Parents who don't give a damn about their kids have always been bad parents. But parents who smother their children, try to control their every action, try to make them into someone they're not, may be even worse.

Children in that second kind of family have the added problem that they're trained to feel guilty if they criticise or seem ungrateful. At least in the first kind of family the children may feel free to express their rage and grief. In the second type the rage and grief will be there but may be hard to express.

Fathers these days are still trying to find a role for themselves. There have always been lots of good fathers, deeply and lovingly involved with their children. But the Anglo culture of the last 50 years didn't support them. A British soldier in 1941 described in the book *Popski's Private Army* how he got ready to join the army. He said he took his two daughters to a boarding school in South Africa, booked them in and, in his own words, 'dismissed them from my mind for the next few years'. He didn't seem bothered by this.

The culture in those times praised men who earned money for their families and supported them in a warm, secure home, so that they weren't hungry or cold or under-clothed or frightened. There was little recognition of men's role in nurturing. Fathers were more likely to shake their sons' hands than hug them.

'He was a good provider' was a common compliment a widow would pay to her husband after he died.

At least nowadays the culture is more likely to support fathers who show that they care, but there are still plenty of fathers who shake hands rather than hug.

However one big improvement for young people is that they have access to more knowledge than previous generations. They live in a more open world, where things are discussed more. A book like this could not have been published a few decades ago.

BAD FATHERS AND NO FATHERS

You need a father.

Some people think they have a father, but they don't.

By 'father' I mean someone who takes a big interest in you, who gives you good advice, who shows his love and respect for you. Someone you can talk to about anything. (That's the kind of father you should aim to be for your kids.)

You might already have a father like that. That's great. If you do, you can skip the rest of this section.

A lot of people don't have fathers any more. Maybe yours died, or maybe he left.

Maybe you have a father but he's part-time – you see him every second weekend, but then sometimes he's busy that weekend, or he's away, or 'Could we make it next weekend, because I've got a whole lot of people coming over on Saturday and I'll hardly have a chance to talk to you . . .' Or you go there and as soon as you arrive he takes you off to a party and you hang around there all night waiting for him to finish and take you home again . . . Or he leaves you home eating pizza and watching TV while he goes off with his girlfriend.

This is irresponsible fathering. Your father can live apart from your mother but he must still be a caring full-time parent.

'Full-time' in the sense that you're never out of his thoughts. He shows it and you know it. You're never out of his caring, interested, loving, respectful thoughts.

Maybe you have a father but he's messed up by drugs or grog.

Your father might be bad-tempered, immature, lacking self-control. He could be violent with his fists or violent with his words. There could be 'something broken inside his head'.

Maybe he treats women without respect, speaking of them abusively, acting violently towards them, using them for sex in an irresponsible, ugly, unloving way.

Maybe he's selfish or greedy or dishonest. Maybe he lies to you. If he cheats other people or lies to them or steals from them, he won't be honest in his dealings with you or your mother or anyone else.

Or his failure as a father mightn't be so obvious. He might be a bad father because he's trying to make you into something you're not. He puts too much pressure on you. He doesn't show any understanding of your ambitions. He criticises you too much. Whatever you do is never good enough.

He mightn't be very interested in you. He could favour your sister or brother over you.

He could spend too much time at work. He works 12 hours a day. He stays back at nights. He works weekends. When you go on a family holiday he leaves early because he has to get back to work.

This father is using work as an excuse to avoid being with you and the other members of your family.

If you think these things are happening, they probably are. It's probably not your imagination. Trust your judgement on this. A bad father doesn't have to be a drunken violent man who beats you up every second day. He might be a quiet polite man, friendly to the neighbours, in a good job. Other people might tell you what a good man he is, even how lucky you are to have him as a father.

This makes it all the more confusing for you, as you try to work out why you're so unhappy with him, why your relationship doesn't seem positive.

So you have a father, supposedly, only he has many serious inadequacies.

A lot of people who don't understand families don't want to believe it can be like this. It makes them angry. 'You should respect your father', they say, as if you should respect someone who's lazy or violent or insensitive.

They say: 'There's too much talk about young people's rights! What about their responsibilities?'

People who talk like this haven't thought things through. They're not prepared to look closely at what's going on. Maybe they're running away from things in their own life that they don't want to know about.

Sure, you have important responsibilities, but you mightn't feel like doing much about them if you live in a family where you're treated as an infant or an idiot, where you're not trusted, where you're not respected and loved. You're probably too angry to feel like putting in much effort around your home.

CHANGING YOUR FATHER

If you have a poor father you might have to put a lot of energy and effort into trying to change him.

It's possible that you can change him. Your best hope is to talk to him at a time when neither of you are stressed. Tell him that you want to talk to him about something very serious. Explain how you feel about these problems. This is a situation where you may have to be more like the parent than your parent. Your mother, if you have one, may be able to help you with advice about how to talk to him.

If you can't talk to him, try writing him a letter.

You may dream that he will change and become the perfect father. Bad luck. That won't happen. He may improve, but he's never going to be the perfect father. Still, if he does improve, you've achieved something very important.

There may also be things you're doing that are making for a bad relationship. If you're lazy around the house. If you sulk instead of telling him what you're angry about. If you show no respect for his feelings. If you're selfish or greedy.

But don't take the whole thing onto your shoulders. And, to make this a bit more complicated, if you're sulky or lazy or selfish or greedy, it may just mean that you're angry and unhappy about what's happening in your family. You feel you can't talk to other family members, or do anything about the problems, so you act badly instead.

If your feelings are trampled on at home you mightn't be too keen to unload the dishwasher or feed the dog or mow the lawn.

If you don't have a father, or you don't have a good father, you need to get one.

GETTING A FATHER

You can adopt a father. Of course he's not really going to be your father. But your 'adopted father' can play an important part in your life.

A lot of guys do this unconsciously. They attach themselves to an older male, in a way that is a bit like a father–son relationship. This is more than just a good idea. It's a powerful – maybe essential – thing for you to do.

The person may be a grandfather, an uncle, an older brother, a godfather. He may be a priest or rabbi or teacher. He may be a friend or the father of a friend.

If there are problems with this relationship, it could mean that you chose badly. You chose someone immature and irresponsible, or abusive. You may have chosen someone with exactly the same problems as your real father.

Generally someone who's only a couple of years older than you won't be very good in this role. They're not yet ready for the responsibilities of parenting.

Problems may also come because you expected too much from this person. You may have thought he was perfect. You may have thought he would be your real father. But of course he can never be that. And of course he is not perfect.

Nevertheless he can help fill a big gap. He can spend time with you, take an interest in you, let you know when you're going down the wrong path, reassure you when you're on the right path.

Make sure you respect his needs too. If it's going to work, it'll have to be a two-way relationship.

The other way you can help make up for the lack of a father is to become your own father. This might sound like a tough gig, but if that's the only way you can do it, fine. The main thing is that you have a father. That's essential.

Being your own father means that you step back and look at your actions from a new point of view. When you're not sure what you're doing, or whether what you're doing is right, ask: 'What would a good father tell me to do, in this situation? What advice would a good father have?'

Then follow the advice.

For example, suppose you have to choose between playing in a semi-final of your squash competition, or going to your cousin's eighteenth birthday. Ask yourself 'What would the good father tell me to do?'

If you're in big trouble at school, about to be suspended maybe, ask yourself: 'What advice would the good father have for me?' The same question applies if you're having a fight with your mother, or you don't know what subjects to pick for school or TAFE or university, or there's a girl you like and you want to get to know her better.

The more you do this the better you get at it, until you become used to looking after yourself and doing what is truly the best for you.

DRUGS

You might sigh as you read the next few paragraphs, and think, 'Oh yeah, here we go again, the same old stuff about drugs being bad for you.'

So, do you want me to change the truth just because you're sick of hearing it?

The point of this book is to tell the truth, whether it's popular or not. There's a lot of misinformation going around. Sometimes people prefer lies, because they think the truth will interfere with their pleasure.

The truth about drugs is easy. They're bad. They're bad for the following reasons:

1. They cause physical and mental damage, some of which can never be repaired.
2. They lead to addiction, which means you've

handed over control of your life to other forces. The mature person controls his own life.

3. They cause loss of control. While you're out of control you can damage yourself and others.
4. The drug culture is a culture of losers. I'm not talking about people who take drugs occasionally. But people who take drugs heavily, daily, are people who have lost the plot. No-one in their right mind really believes that drugs are where it's at. The more you take drugs the more time you spend hanging around with losers. One of the neat tricks with drugs is that they give you the feeling you're superior because 'Wow, I've taken drugs (heroin for example) and all those boring ordinary people haven't'. If this is the way you get to feel superior, you have a big problem with confidence.
5. When you buy drugs you're supporting criminals. By giving them money you're encouraging them to trap other people, sometimes causing their death.
6. There is no creativity in drugs.

Most people who use drugs offer these excuses to themselves:

1. Adults set us a bad example by smoking and drinking and taking prescription drugs so they

can't complain if we take drugs (as if the weakness of these adults means it's OK for you to be weak too).

2. My parents took all kinds of drugs when they were younger, and they've survived. (Your parents may be immature in their role as parents. Don't model yourself on their weak behaviour and their past mistakes.)
3. Reality sucks – I'd rather take drugs (try changing your reality – drugs are a surrender to the reality that you don't like. You've let the reality defeat you).
4. A little bit won't hurt (all drugs cause damage).
5. It just happens so easily at parties . . . everyone's using stuff, and before I know it I am too. It happens in a way that doesn't make it seem like a big deal, even though I was always so sure I'd never get into that. (If you haven't got the strength of character to say no, invent an excuse for why you can't take them. Say you have asthma or you're allergic or you have such bad trips you can't take them any more. Avoid parties like that in the first place. Go with a friend or partner who you can trust to help you avoid trying drugs. Fake it – pretend to take them. But afterwards, find some new friends.)

Some people take drugs as a way of telling their parents to get stuffed. They're saying, through the drugs, that they reject the lifestyle and values of their parents.

It would be more effective to tell your parents this than to do yourself terrible damage by telling them so indirectly. You must feel very threatened by them, dominated by them, under their shadow, that you can communicate with them only in this way. You've got a lot of work ahead of you to resolve all this.

I've known a lot of people who've gotten into the drug scene in a big way. They've all been people with serious emotional problems – problems of unhappiness, anger, loneliness, feelings of failure, lack of confidence. Mostly they haven't realised the seriousness of their own problems. They are people who have learnt not to talk about their problems, who maintain a mask which hides their deep and extreme sadness. By refusing to look at those problems, by turning to drugs instead, they've condemned themselves to terrible damage, in some cases to death.

In other words, many men are so unable to talk about their problems that they would rather destroy themselves than talk.

Is talking that painful?

True friends would help you talk about your problems and help you resolve them, rather than push drugs onto you.

If you feel the need to take drugs, you have

problems in your life that you're not coping with. Get some help with those problems, as a matter of urgency. Quit running.

Despite this, nearly all the readers of this book will try drugs: at least nicotine, alcohol and dope. You can survive light use of these without serious damage. Addiction to any of them will be a disaster for you. Some people have addictive personalities, which means they become addicted very easily and quickly. If you think this sounds like you, take great care of yourself.

Recognise that the drug stage of your life is an immature stage. The fact that some adults stay in this stage forever doesn't make it any less immature. Try to move through the drug stage quickly and get up to the next level, where you take on responsibilities and take charge of your own life. It's more interesting, rewarding and satisfying.

PUBERTY

Puberty for boys can begin at ages 11 through 17. The age of puberty is dropping quite fast, possibly because of better health and food, possibly because of the growth hormones farmers now feed to their stock, which are still in the food when we eat it.

Some boys can't wait to get to puberty; others are nervous of it, reluctant to grow up. I suspect that someone who is extremely anxious about puberty can actually delay getting there, by the power of their mind, but I don't know of any medical evidence for that theory.

I've known a few boys who didn't reach puberty until they were in Year 12. That can be a tough gig. Several were fine about it, several felt unhappy that they weren't keeping up with their friends.

Boys who reach puberty at a young age are bigger and stronger than their friends for a while but are often shorter than average as adults.

Here's how to tell if you've 'officially' reached puberty:

1. Once the testicles reach a certain size, you have officially begun puberty. As a medical fact, the circumference of the testicles is a certain guide to the onset of puberty.
2. There is a theory that when the hair around your penis becomes wavy, you've reached puberty.
3. Most males think of their first ejaculation as the moment of reaching puberty.

Here are the physical changes of puberty:

THE PENIS: becomes longer and thicker. Average size varies as much as the size of noses vary, or the size and shape of bodies vary. It's said that the average size of an adult penis, when soft, is around 6 to 12 cms, and when hard between 12 and 18 cms. But it's doubtful that anyone's ever done a major survey of them.

There's never been a male who wasn't interested in the size and shape of his penis. With some emotionally unhappy males it becomes an obsession. Every sex education book ever written will tell you that size isn't important. Medically speaking, that's true. A small penis performs exactly the same as a medium or large penis.

If size and shape do matter, it's because of attitudes. There are lots of jokes about penis size, and males who want to put other males down will make jokes suggesting that the other man has a small penis. Some women say they find a large penis more exciting when they're having sex. Others say a large penis makes them uncomfortable. Both statements could be correct; both could be more to do with psychological reasons.

Males with small penises tend not to feel proud of their penis size. They might have to look elsewhere for sources of pride. Be aware though of the 'foreshortening' effect: when you look down at your penis it will appear smaller, simply because of the angle from which you're looking at it.

Some males with big penises feel proud, some embarrassed. It's odd that people should feel proud or embarrassed about something they have no control over.

Your penis will get smaller when it's cold. Both the penis and the scrotum (ball bag) shrivel a little, and draw back into the body for protection.

Penis size can't be changed, except by serious plastic surgery. Men who are interested in having surgery like that have a big problem with their confidence.

In recent years women have come to realise

how much their body shape and size have been used for centuries to make them feel bad. Girls and women have been made to feel that everything depends on how they look. If they're above or below average weight, or if their breasts are large or small, they're sometimes made to feel that they've failed as human beings.

The fact is that the same thing happens to men. Boys or men who are above or below average weight, who have ears or lips or a nose or a penis that is unique to them, are often teased and made to feel there is something wrong with them. This can do terrible and long-lasting damage.

If you feel that your penis (or anything else about your body) is the wrong size or shape, you probably have a confidence problem. You may have a lot of work ahead of you to fix this problem. It is extremely unhelpful for you to abuse yourself: to tell yourself how fat or skinny or ugly or grotesque you are. This is a very damaging and dangerous thing to do.

TESTICLES: these two balls, which hang in a bag called the scrotum, drop lower and get bigger as puberty continues. As with the penis, the scrotum comes in a variety of sizes and shapes. It's entirely normal for one testicle to hang lower than the other. It's entirely normal for the scrotum to have freckles or brown spots, but of course as with any spot on the body, if these change colour or get bigger or bleed you should see a doctor immediately.

Sometimes one or both testicles didn't drop properly when you were a baby, but got caught up in the abdomen. This is easily fixed but should be fixed straight away, and will require you to see a doctor.

ERECTIONS: erections are when your penis sticks up stiff and firm. It's a rush of blood to the penis that makes it go like that.

The reason you have them is so that the penis can enter the vagina, on its way to deliver sperm to the woman's egg. Unless it's stiff it won't go into the vagina.

Most boys have erections through their childhood years. Some baby boys are actually born with an erection.

The erections you have when you're little can be to do with sex: seeing someone naked, having someone play with your penis, seeing animals have sex, watching an R-rated video for example. But they can be nothing to do with sex. Being nervous in class, riding in the car, watching an exciting movie, going to the Show . . . anything can cause your penis to react.

I remember reading years ago about a young boy who had an erection as he watched a time-lapse film of a flower unfurling.

The erections you have when you're a kid can feel nice and exciting. Or they can make you nervous and uncomfortable. Or both, at different times. And some boys don't seem to have erections until they're close to puberty.

A common cause of erections, in boys, adolescents and men, is the desire to urinate. So many boys and men wake up with erections every morning that they're actually called 'morning erections', and they're usually caused by the desire to go to the bathroom. The easiest way to get that erection down is to take a leak. Other ways to get erections to go down are to think of something else, to start an activity that will take all your attention, to get into a conversation that isn't about sex. The old-fashioned remedy was the cold shower. Certainly erections don't like cold, but it's a pretty drastic remedy. I'd rather have the erection.

Fear will usually cause an erection to go down, but it's not recommended either.

You normally can only ejaculate if your penis is erect. And you normally can't urinate through a totally erect penis. It'll have to come down a little bit at least. You might find the urine then sprays around, so you have to do some mopping up if you've missed the bowl. It's really crass to leave that task to someone else.

As you enter puberty erections become a more powerful part of your life. Chances are you'll have them more often, and the feelings from them will be a lot stronger. For quite a while though, as in childhood, they'll probably be caused by all kinds of things, not just sex. I had an erection almost every morning from the rocking of the school bus, through Years 8, 9, 10 . . . I enjoyed it, although it made getting off the bus a bit awkward, and potentially embarrassing.

Of course with your penis getting bigger your erections get bigger too. A character in my book *The Great Gatenby* is supposed to be able to hang five towels from his erection. This is sheer fantasy on my part, although there may be guys with erections that big.

It's quite normal for erections to be more horizontal than vertical. As you get older they'll get more horizontal anyway. It's equally normal for an erection to be so vertical it touches your stomach. As usual, each person's different, although the more excited you are, and the longer time it's been since you last ejaculated, the bigger and more vertical your penis is likely to be.

Your erection might lean to the right or to the left or go straight up and down; these are usually all normal, although some leans can be the result of a medical condition which it's worth having a doctor check.

If you have an erection as part of a sexual experience, like masturbating or kissing or petting, the longer that experience lasts the more your erection is likely to change. It'll probably become darker in colour, throb more noticeably, and semen will 'leak' from it. It'll probably become bigger and stiffer. On the other hand, if the sexual experience goes on for a long time, your penis may need a rest, and go soft again for a while.

There's an expression 'lover's balls', which refers to the fact that a guy who's had an erection for a while and hasn't ejaculated will feel the pressure in his penis and testicles, which may well become more swollen, and darker in colour. Over the centuries many guys have used this feeling of pressure in their erection as an excuse to get girls to have sex with them. 'I'll die if I don't have it!' 'You've got to let me; I swear, it's killing me.'

If you do die in these circumstances you'll make medical history. It hasn't happened yet. To be so worked up and have to settle for less than intercourse – for example, masturbating – can be extremely disappointing. But to use that as an excuse for rape, as some sad men have done over the years, is to deny your responsibilities as an adult.

SEMEN: the first ejaculation can be difficult to identify, because some boys have a few drops of white or colourless liquid 'leaking' from their penis for a few weeks or months before their first real ejaculation. Some boys ejaculate a small amount of colourless liquid a number of times. Gradually it becomes more obviously semen, in its colour and quantity.

Semen is usually a milky white colour, not as liquid as water, more like shampoo, but it can be quite thin and runny sometimes. It contains the sperm which fertilises the woman's eggs to make babies. The amount, colour, and the force with which semen comes out vary from person to person, and are also affected by how long your penis has been excited before the ejaculation, how sexually excited you are by the situation you're in and how recently you have had other ejaculations.

Normally the semen is ejaculated with great force, so that it can reach the woman's uterus and the sperm can fertilise an egg.

Semen has its own smell and taste, usually quite subtle. Some people find its smell and taste off-putting, some find it sexually exciting.

Semen doesn't stain: it washes out of clothes and sheets easily. It is safe to taste and swallow.

You may notice that the first urination after an ejaculation is a bit wild. The urine, which comes out of the same tiny hole as the semen, might spray around in a few different directions. This is just because there's still a drop or two of semen clogging the hole.

WET DREAMS: in adolescence most boys have exciting dreams often or sometimes, during which the penis gets stiff and ejaculates while they're asleep. The dreams are usually about sex, but they can be unusual: for example you might dream about having sex with a super-model, or a child, or you dream that your grandmother is masturbating you, or that a guy is sucking your penis.

Don't panic! These situations (except for the super-model one!) might have you wondering about yourself. But it's entirely normal for you to have all kinds of unconventional dreams about sex.

You often have wet dreams when you haven't had an ejaculation for a while. Often only a small amount of semen is ejaculated, but again that varies from person to person, from day to day.

BONE AND MUSCLES: the growth that begins at puberty continues for many years. Most men are well into their twenties before they are fully grown. It's true of muscle that 'if you don't use it you lose it'. Health, strength and co-ordination all improve with exercise.

In the early stages of adolescence however it's important not to strain the body by asking too much of it. Trying to lift enormous weights, for example, is dangerous. On the other hand it's good to test yourself to the limits, to see how strong and fast and fit you are. A short course of training can cause amazing improvement. Get advice from a P.E. teacher or a coach.

HAIR: hair grows on the face, under the arms, around the penis, and in some men on the chest and on the back.

The hair around the penis gradually forms into a triangle pointing upwards. In women the hair on the vulva gradually forms into a triangle pointing downwards.

A line of hair, sometimes called the 'flea track', appears from the bellybutton to the groin.

The hair on the arms and legs that children have from birth becomes darker and longer and rougher.

The hair on the head has a different texture to the hair on the rest of the body, but the colour is usually similar.

You should be concerned if your parents are reluctant to get you a razor when you obviously need one. It may be that they do not want to notice that you have reached puberty. If this is the case you may have a problem establishing your independence in the years ahead.

VOICE: the change in the voice begins some time after puberty and continues for a long time. The voice can break suddenly or gradually. Sometimes a young man will have a croaky or unreliable voice (switching from high to low or low to high) for a while. But if a young man's voice continues to be squeaky or strained for a long time there may be a physical or emotional cause. Check it out with a doctor or speech therapist.

I had a friend who had a very croaky and nasal voice all through adolescence. He was so embarrassed about it that he hardly talked to anyone and avoided girls. When he was 24 a doctor realised he had an adenoid problem that caused his voice to sound unusual. He had a small operation which fixed it completely. The change in his personality was absolutely amazing. I thought it was sad that he'd gone through those years of unnecessary suffering.

Again, it would have been better if his confidence hadn't depended so much on his voice, but I know it's easy for me to say that, and not always so easy in real life.

Most men's voices don't become fully mature until they're in their twenties.

Some people say that if you want a good singing voice as a man you should be careful not to push your voice too hard as an adolescent, by trying to reach notes that are beyond you, or by shouting or screaming so hard that you damage your voice. Certainly it is possible to cause permanent damage.

SWEAT: as an adolescent you may sweat more than at any other stage of your life. Gradually the body starts to settle down again and sweat levels stabilise. In the meantime though you may be embarrassed by sweating a lot, or by hurtful jokes about smelly feet.

It seems that a lot of people think adolescent males have no feelings, that these insulting jokes don't do any harm. Some boys aren't upset by them, but some are, and they have a right to be.

On the other hand, during these years of high sweat levels, you should have the respect for yourself, and the consideration for others, to shower when necessary and to use deodorants.

Some deodorants are made especially for men and some for women, and some are for anyone. Try to avoid deodorants with aluminium, as these may be harmful if used for many years. Read the fine print on the container when you're in the supermarket or chemist's.

THE CHEST: many adolescent males – as many as 80 per cent – develop some fat in the chest area, which may look a bit like breasts in a girl. Again this can lead to embarrassment and teasing. This stage of growth doesn't last long: the fat soon goes away again.

For a short time it may even be possible for some boys to squeeze a drop of clear liquid from a nipple during puberty, but this doesn't mean anything. It's just another example of the body going through this unsettled period of change.

The nipples usually get bigger with puberty, and more 'active': boys find that their nipples can produce exciting feelings, not as powerful as the feelings from the penis, but nice. The nipples on males and females do erect when they're excited: they become like stiff little buttons. For most males the penis is the most sexually exciting part of the body, followed by the nipples and buttocks.

GROWTH SPURT: you can grow dramatically during puberty, putting on a number of centimetres in just a few months. Then you might plateau for a while, before another quick growth.

Or you might just grow at a steady rate. Or you mightn't get a lot taller than you were before puberty. But the size you were before puberty has no relationship to the size you will be as an adult. It's genetically programmed. It's not affected by smoking or drugs or masturbation or exercise.

It's now believed that if your father is more than four and a half centimetres taller than your mother you will grow to be taller than her.

You will end up with your shoulders wider than your hips, unlike girls, who when they finish growing have hips wider than their shoulders. Don't be surprised though if you put on some fat for a few years during puberty. It may be that you're eating wrongly or that you're unfit, but it may also be just a natural side-effect of puberty.

ACNE: sometimes the skin does break out during adolescence, usually not until you're well into puberty. To read some ads in magazines you'd think it's the only big issue of adolescence.

Again it's often a question of confidence how well you handle a big outbreak of acne. Generally people who refuse to be trampled on, who refuse to be pushed aside, don't get trampled on or pushed aside. People who have the confidence to be at the centre of a group, at a party for example, are accepted on their own terms, whether they have acne or not. After a very short time no-one notices the acne. It's like, when you meet someone, you might notice they have a birthmark on the side of their face. You notice it the same way you notice the colour of their hair, the slogan on their T-shirt, the way they talk. Then you forget about those things as you get to know them better.

It's the same with acne and all those other things you wish you didn't have, like a stammer or a big nose or puppy fat. They're all part of you, they contribute to the unique you.

After all, do you really want to be friends with someone who'd judge you on stuff like that?

Comedian Groucho Marx had a famous line: 'I wouldn't want to belong to the kind of club that'd have me as a member.' I suggest you shouldn't want to belong to the kind of club that has people who judge you on surface things like acne.

Nevertheless if you get a big hit of acne, check with your doctor for the latest treatment. If he or she doesn't seem up to date, or doesn't have many ideas, go to another doctor.

THINKING: before or during puberty the brain begins to operate in new ways. For many boys this means that they start to think in abstract terms for the first time in their lives. By abstract thinking, we mean that you understand more than the obvious.

Children generally only understand what they see and touch. They can understand ideas if they are explained in language that is basic, using lots of practical examples.

People who think in abstract terms though can understand ideas and explore them using abstract language.

If you take a topic like war, the abstract thinker might consider issues like 'Why people fight', 'Whether it is human nature to fight', 'Whether it is permissible to kill other people during a war', 'Whether a war can ever be justified', 'How war can be discouraged'.

People who are not abstract thinkers are more likely to see wars in terms of goodies and baddies. They understand war best in terms of stories. They are easily manipulated by governments, who excite them with simple slogans, emotional speeches about dead warriors and photos of leaders looking heroic and enemy leaders looking evil.

People who are not abstract thinkers see life in terms of goodies and baddies. Television programmes like *A Current Affair* and *60 Minutes* are designed for such people. Politicians tend to aim their campaigns at them.

People who think in abstractions often have the greatest difficulty getting on with people who don't. And vice versa. They just don't understand each other. 'Can't you follow simple logic?' pleads the abstract thinker. 'Why do you have to make everything so complicated?' groans the other.

SEX

Your penis doesn't rule the world. It isn't the most important thing in the world. Nor is it the most powerful. But when you reach puberty you may think it is. It takes a while to get used to the fact that it's bigger, it gets hard more often, and it can ejaculate. It feels extremely powerful.

The feelings you get from it are on a different level to the feelings you got before puberty.

Many males never grow out of the stage of thinking their penis is the most important thing in the world. They spend their whole life obsessed by it.

This can show in a number of ways. They talk endlessly about sex. They think every girl is as fascinated by their penis as they are. Their jokes are often about penises. They might even constantly scratch themselves there.

Sometimes this fascination shows up in less obvious ways. Men can be strongly attracted to things that seem like penises to them, at an unconscious level. If men are into guns in an obsessive way, or in love with fast powerful cars, that probably means they're still at the penis stage of development.

Becoming a mature man means recognising that your penis is not the most powerful tool you have. Your intelligence, your strength, your creative skills, your sense of humour, your good taste and judgement: these are more important and more powerful than your penis.

Old legends sometimes give messages to boys about how they should grow up sexually.

For instance, the Jack and the Beanstalk story is really about Jack becoming a mature man. At puberty Jack throws his magic seeds (sperm) onto the ground, where they grow into an enormous beanstalk (like the way most guys unconsciously think of their penis after puberty, when it usually grows much bigger). Jack climbs the beanstalk three times. The first time he comes back with golden eggs. He thinks that's all he needs: he can now live happily ever after. He believes that one lucky strike is enough to set him up for life. Nothing else matters.

At this stage Jack is still very immature. He's like the man who buys lottery tickets or goes gambling: believing that sooner or later he'll strike it rich. He doesn't need to work to get anywhere. You know some men like this.

Later Jack realises he's not satisfied with just the golden eggs. He needs something more. He goes up the stalk again and comes back with the golden goose. Now he's getting somewhere. He's recognised that he's got to have money coming in all the time. He can't just rely on one lucky strike, like gambling or an inheritance. He has to have regular income, like you get from a job, or from farming the land.

Then Jack makes one more trip up the beanstalk. He kills the giant and comes back with the golden harp.

He's now mature. He has not only defeated his father; he's realised that art and music and literature (represented by the golden harp) are more important than money. The truly mature person understands that. Jack can now cut down the beanstalk. He knows that his penis is not the biggest or most important thing in his life after all. There's more to life than his penis. He's become a true adult.

BEING GAY

Most guys wonder from time to time if they might be gay. Especially during adolescence.

Some guys know from a very early age that they are gay. Others are not sure for a long time.

All males are attracted to other males in some ways. All honest males will agree that they can recognise beauty in other males, that they'll quite often notice the good looks of another male.

All males are interested to see other guys in the nude when they're growing up, to see what they look like, to compare with their own bodies. They may feel excited at the sight of other males naked, getting an erection for example.

That's got nothing to do with being gay.

Many boys play with each other's bodies when they're young, feeling penises, masturbating, having sex games. Playing these games with other boys has got nothing to do with being gay either.

But they may think it does. Some guys who have had a happy, normal childhood suddenly fall apart during adolescence, becoming depressed and suicidal, unable to talk to anyone about it. Often it's because they believe they are gay.

It's understandable that for some guys this is a huge issue, and it throws them into a bad state of mind. They fear that if they are gay their families will freak out, their friends will dump them, their social life will die overnight, they'll attract abuse, they'll become freaks. They're depressed by, amongst other things, the thought that they'll never become fathers themselves. They see their life ahead as a horrible unpleasant experience.

If you're in this situation, the first thing to say is that you may be gay or you may not be.

If you are gay you may be relaxed and happy about it. But it's true that being gay is still a tough gig for many guys. The good news however is that it's getting easier all the time. The world is changing fast. In a few more years, at the present rate of change, being gay won't be an issue.

The gay community is, for the most part, a caring, supportive, friendly one. All its members went through what you're going through now, and they do understand. Instead of letting your mind run wild thinking about how awful life's going to be, maybe you should think about how, by showing courage, you can help accelerate the improvement in the lives of gay people. There's a lot of new friends out there waiting to meet you and support you.

Gay Sex

Whether it's sex with females or sex with males, the same rules apply. Act with integrity. Sex should be a loving act between two people who have made a serious commitment to each other. Cheating, lying, betrayal, casual sex are always bad karma. Trust, generosity, respect are always good karma.

When gay men have sex, they use as much

variety as when men and women have sex: using hands, mouths, genitals. The most controversial aspect of gay sex is anal sex, where one man puts his penis into the anus (the ass) of the other. Many people think that if you're gay, anal sex goes with the territory, automatically.

That's not the case. Many gay men never have anal sex.

If you do have anal sex you must use condoms, because of the danger of AIDS. You must be careful the condom doesn't break or come off. For some men anal sex can be uncomfortable or painful, especially the first few times. For others it's no problem.

MASTURBATION

Most guys masturbate, but it's not compulsory. If you prefer not to, that's fine.

Some people masturbate a lot, some only occasionally. After you reach puberty, masturbation normally ends in a climax, with semen shooting out. But not always. Sometimes you can have a 'dry run', where there's a lesser climax and no semen.

If you haven't masturbated or had a wet dream or had sex for a while, you'll probably shoot out more semen, with greater force. After a lot of ejaculations the amount of semen might reduce to a few drops. The body always recovers however. You'll never run out of semen.

People will tell you that masturbation can't hurt you. That's more or less true, but it's a bit more complicated than that. If you masturbate too much, for example, you'll notice all kinds of effects. You might get tired and bad-tempered, lose strength and energy. These effects won't last long, but they are signals from your body that you're overdoing it. Too much of anything is a bad idea, and that includes masturbating.

Further, boys who spend a lot of time masturbating might be having problems with relationships. Because they are nervous about mixing with people, or meeting new people, or they feel lonely, or they're anxious about girls, they stay in their bedrooms and masturbate. Boys in this situation need to be working on the reasons they feel scared of people, instead of pushing their problems away.

When you masturbate, don't always do it the same way. Use imagination and variety. That'll help you have a better sex life when you're with a partner. Otherwise you might end up only able to be aroused in a narrow range of ways.

Don't always rush to get it over with. Take your time. Your partner will probably enjoy sex with you more if you're able to hold back your climax for a while. If you get used to always having quick ejaculations when you masturbate, you mightn't find it so easy to delay them, later, when you really want to.

Treat your body, especially your genitals, with respect.

HAVING SEX

The amount of fun and pleasure you get from sex will depend on how much effort you put into making it good for both of you. This applies equally to gay sex and straight sex. To be bothered only with your own pleasure is selfish, but ironically you suffer as well. The sex isn't as good for you either.

Foreplay is the name given to the stuff people do with each other before they move towards their orgasms or climaxes – for instance, before the man actually puts his penis in the vagina.

As a general rule the longer the foreplay the more exciting the sex is for both people. And the more creative you are with foreplay, the better. Explore each other's bodies, find the things that your partner really enjoys, tell her or him what you enjoy.

A problem for a male can be that he gets so excited during the foreplay that he ejaculates. For most males this means there'll be some time before he's able to get another erection, or ejaculate again. So an early ejaculation can put an end to the good time he and his partner were having.

If it looks like you and your partner might go all the way with sex you're going to have to do something about pregnancy and/or AIDS. Even if you're not going all the way you might have to do something. For example, if you put your penis in your partner's vagina and take it out again without ejaculating, you might have already made her pregnant, given her AIDS or caught AIDS yourself. Semen can leak out of your penis all the time when you're turned on, and that's all it takes.

If you and your partner are having anal sex, again AIDS is a danger. You can also catch AIDS through contact between the penis and the mouth, but that's less common.

I've deliberately avoided having whole big sections of this book about stuff like AIDS and the STDs (sexually transmitted diseases) like herpes, syphilis, gonorrhoea. Likewise I haven't gone into a whole lot of detail about things that can go wrong with the penis or scrotum, or sex generally. That's because I don't want to make sex sound like some minefield: one foot wrong and you go up in flames. There's enough – far too much – tension about sex already, for most people. It should be obvious to you if there's something wrong: like blood in your urine, pus coming out of your penis, pain when you take a leak. All these things happen occasionally to some guys; all are symptoms of infections; all can be cured: just take yourself to a doctor.

Anyway, back to pregnancy and AIDS. For sex involving the vagina or the anus we're talking condoms. There are other ways of birth control or dealing with unwanted pregnancy, like the Pill, 'morning after' tablets, diaphragms, and the rhythm method (all controlled by the woman), abortion after the woman gets pregnant, and vasectomy for the man, but this book isn't really the place to deal with them.

Condoms are a different matter though, as in modern times all guys should know about them and be willing and able to use them. For one thing they are the best way of preventing AIDS, and they have a success rate in the 90 per cent range for preventing pregnancy. Please remember that they're not perfect though. If they break while you're in your partner, you're back to where you were before.

You can buy condoms in chemists, but if you're embarrassed by that, you can buy them in supermarkets, or from vending machines in some public places, like toilets in pubs or at airports. They cost $1 each from a vending machine.

Condoms are easy to put on as long as you have an erection. Make sure they haven't been tampered with by one of your friends. Boys who are nervous about sex sometimes show it in their excited reactions to their friends having sex: spying on you, or banging on a door to try to disturb you. Or putting pinpricks in your condoms.

It's a good idea to practise putting on a condom some time when you're masturbating, so when you use one with a partner you'll be able to put it on without any hassles.

Condoms can break and they can come off. If you're using them, the most important thing is that you have to take your penis out of the other person once you've ejaculated. If you wait, your penis will (usually) go soft again, and because it becomes smaller the condom slips off.

Condoms come in only one size. You can buy different varieties of them, and different colours, as well as some with contours. These are supposed to give the woman better feelings inside the vagina, but for most women they don't seem to make much difference.

A couple of other points about having sex with girls:

The vagina doesn't itself give very exciting feelings. This helps explain why to some women and girls the part of sex where the penis is in the vagina – which to guys is often the best part – isn't necessarily their favourite. If you want to be a good lover you'll be aware of that, and make sure you give your partner pleasure in other ways. Her face, her breasts, her legs, her genitals, every part of her body can give her wonderful feelings. The difference between a guy who's a good lover and a guy who's a bad lover is as simple as that: better lovers are ready and willing to spend time exciting their partner.

The vagina needs to be wet for the penis to be able to enter easily. Normally this happens naturally: the girl who is sexually excited begins to get moist. The wetness then lubricates the vagina, so the penis can slide in and out more easily.

All the jokes about Vaseline and masturbation refer to the fact that Vaseline on your penis feels a bit like the wetness of a girl's vagina.

If the wetness doesn't happen, it may be because the two of you didn't spend enough time in foreplay, or she's too nervous, or she just isn't someone who gets a lot of wetness happening. No problem. You can use a cream of some kind. Experiment with what you find in the bathroom cupboard. Don't use nail polish. Or you can buy stuff like KY-JELLY from a chemist.

When women have an orgasm it's often not as obvious as when a man has one (he usually ejaculates semen). The female orgasm can include violent shuddering, shaking, trembling, spasms, crying out, even fainting. Boys who haven't reached puberty can still have orgasms, and they are quite similar to female ones, but often their penis is involved as well – it might throb or shudder.

A female orgasm may last for longer than a male one – maybe a minute or more.

MYTHS ABOUT SEX

1. A male and female can become locked together during sex, and they have to be taken to hospital in the back of an ambulance, to be separated.

THE TRUTH: this is impossible for humans. It can happen in some animal species but not in humans. It is true though that some women can be so nervous about sex that it is not possible for the man to get entry to her vagina, but the myth about people being locked together probably started because of some people's deep fear of sex. This may have led them to imagine all kinds of frightening situations, including this one.

2. The size of the nose or the hands or some other part of the body shows the size of the penis. Or the size of the mouth or some other part of the body shows the size of the vagina.

THE TRUTH: there's no truth in this at all. You may as well say that the size of the earhole shows the size of the bellybutton.

3. Girls don't think about sex or don't like sex or don't want to have sex.

THE TRUTH: some girls do, some don't, most are somewhere in between. Just like guys. It's not generally admitted that there are guys too who don't think about sex much, don't like sex and don't want sex.

Some people feel under pressure to start dating early, to have sex early. The funny thing is that if you go to a co-ed school you'll notice that very few of the people in your year group are in a serious big-time relationship. Most students finish their five or six years of secondary schooling without having been in a major relationship. Most of them will go for some more time yet before getting into such a relationship. The pressure you feel is not rational. The 11-year-olds on American TV sitcoms who are dating already are the figments of Hollywood imaginations.

4. When a girl says 'No' to sex, that's it, absolutely.

THE TRUTH: this is a controversial issue. In any situation, including sex, 'No' isn't necessarily final. It depends on the 'No'. If a girl says 'No way in the world am I having sex with you', that sounds pretty final to me. If she says 'Oh no no, I really shouldn't', and then kisses you passionately with her mouth open, I'd say, 'Don't give up just yet.'

If you can't tell the difference between an absolute 'No', and a flirting 'No', then you're not mature enough to be having sex. If you ignore an absolute 'No', and keep going, that's rape. You've just ruined her life and yours – for the sake of a couple of minutes of sex. For the sake of one orgasm. That's bad Maths, bad karma, bad sex, being a bad human.

If she says an absolute 'No' but shows some sympathy and understanding, you could try for a compromise. Maybe she'll masturbate you instead. If you completely misjudged the situation and she doesn't want any sexual contact, then go home and masturbate yourself.

If she says 'No' and you go ahead and have sex with her, don't bother coming to me the next day and saying 'Oh, but I didn't think she meant it.'

I'll call you a liar. You know whether she means it or not. If you're genuinely not sure whether she does or doesn't, then stop right there. If in doubt, stop. Put some value on your life and hers. Take care of you both. If you don't like her enough to do that, then take care of yourself. Don't throw away your career, your self-respect, your reputation, your chance for happiness, in exchange for an ejaculation that lasts ten or twenty seconds.

There are lots of other myths about sex, but not many of them are believed nowadays. In case you're wondering though, the following are all rubbish: masturbation causes pimples, blindness, madness, etc etc; Gladwrap makes a good condom; a girl can't get pregnant the first time she has sex; a girl can't get pregnant when she's having her period; a girl can't get pregnant when she's been raped; a girl can't get pregnant if you have sex standing up; you can catch AIDS or VD from a toilet seat; you can tell if a guy's gay by his voice, his hand gestures, whether he can whistle or not, etc etc.

GLOSSARY

It struck me for the first time as I wrote this glossary just how ugly are nearly all our slang words for sex. It seems that many people see sex in ugly abusive terms. It's strange and sad that something which should be so beautiful, so wonderful, such a happy and exciting part of being human, is something that makes many people tense or aggressive.

Sometimes people talk so much about AIDS and STDs and pregnancy that you end up being nervous of sex. These people are often nervous of sex themselves, and they use stuff like AIDS to make other people frightened of sex too. Of course AIDS is a serious problem, to be taken seriously, but keep it in perspective. Don't let it put you off. Wear a condom and don't have sex with people who don't look after themselves. That's all you need to do.

OFFICIAL NAME	MEANING	SLANG WORDS
ABORTION	ending a pregnancy by getting rid of the embryo (the unborn baby, still in the womb)	
ANUS	the hole through which faeces come out	asshole
BESTIALITY	humans having sex with animals	
BISEXUAL	someone sexually attracted to both male and female	AC-DC, bi
BREASTS	bosom; a woman's two organs for milk	boobs, tits, jugs, knockers, melons
BROTHEL	a place where prostitutes work	cat-house
BUTTOCKS	cheeks of the bottom	bum cheeks
CAESAREAN	a baby is born by the doctor operating into the mother's womb, through the stomach, and bringing the baby out that way, instead of the baby making its own way out through the vagina	

OFFICIAL NAME	MEANING	SLANG WORDS
CASTRATION	having the testicles (balls) cut off	gelding
CIRCUMCISION	cutting off the foreskin of the penis	
CLIMAX	the 'explosion' that comes at the end of some sexual activity: for a sexually mature male, this usually means the ejaculation of semen. For women, girls, and boys who haven't reached puberty, it can take many forms, such as violent shuddering, shaking, trembling, spasms, crying out, even fainting	getting your rocks off, coming
CLITORIS	the little bump at the top of the vulva, like a little penis	clit
COITUS	sexual intercourse	see intercourse
COITUS INTERRUPTUS	taking the penis out of the vagina before the male ejaculates	getting off at Redfern (not used much any more), pulling out
CONDOM	latex 'skin' put over the penis to catch the semen, and stop it going into the other person's vagina or anus	prophylactic, French letter, Frenchie, rubber, sheath, franger

OFFICIAL NAME	MEANING	SLANG WORDS
COPULATION	sexual intercourse	see intercourse
CUNNILINGUS	kissing and tonguing a woman's genital area	go down, eat pussy
EJACULATION	the semen shooting out of the penis when a sexually mature male has a climax	shooting
ERECTION	when the penis stands up firm and stiff	stiffy, hard-on, rod, boner, bone, crack a bone, crack a fat, horn
EUNUCH	male who has had both testicles (balls) cut off	
EXHIBITIONISM	sexual excitement some men get from showing their penis to girls or women	flashing (jokes about men in raincoats or macs usually refer to this practice)
FAECES	solid waste passed through the anus	shit, poo, number twos, crap, turd
FELLATIO	sucking on a penis	blow job, sucking off, head job, go down on
FOREPLAY	the way people excite each other sexually before the penis goes into the vagina or anus	
FORESKIN	the piece of skin that covers the tip of the penis; sometimes removed by circumcision	

OFFICIAL NAME	MEANING	SLANG WORDS
GENITALS	the sexual parts of the body: penis and scrotum in men, vagina, clitoris, vulva in women	private parts
GLANS	head of the penis	
GONORRHOEA	See STDs	
HERPES	See STDs	
HOMOSEXUAL	someone who is more sexually attracted to the same gender as themselves	queer, faggot, gay, poofter, nancy, pansy, fag, fruit, queen, (a 'closet gay' is someone who is secretive about being homosexual)
HYMEN	membrane at the entrance to the vagina, that sometimes has to be penetrated before the girl can take a penis into the vagina for the first time	cherry, maidenhead
HYSTERECTOMY	removal of the woman's womb by a doctor, for medical reasons e.g. cancer	
INCEST	sex with close relatives	
INTERCOURSE	actually the word means 'talking, communication'. But it's usually used	fucking, making love, screw, root, having it off, banging, balling, roll in the hay, a

OFFICIAL NAME	MEANING	SLANG WORDS
INTERCOURSE *(continued)*	to mean sexual intercourse, which is sex where the penis is inserted in the vagina	naughty, getting your end in, a lay, a poke
LESBIAN	a woman who is more sexually attracted to women than to men	lemon, gay, lezzo, dyke, butch
LUBRICANT	in this context, oil to help the penis enter the vagina or anus	
MASTURBATE	any use of the hands to excite the genitals, either alone or with someone else	wank, toss off, jerk, pull, hand job, Mrs Palm and her five daughters, beating the meat, jack off, spanking the monkey
MENARCHE	the age at which a girl starts having periods	
MENOPAUSE	when women stop having periods – usually around the age of 50	change of life
MENSTRUATION	bleeding every 28-35 days, by women or adolescent girls, through the vagina	monthlies, the curse, on her rags, that time of the month, women's troubles
NECROPHILIA	being sexually excited by dead people	
NYMPHOMANIAC	a woman who wants sex all the time	

OFFICIAL NAME	MEANING	SLANG WORDS
ORGASM	see climax	see climax
OVUM/OVA	egg produced by woman; when fertilised by sperm it becomes a baby	
PAD	see sanitary napkin	see sanitary napkin
PAEDOPHILIA	being sexually attracted to children	chickenhawk (jokes about boiled lollies usually refer to men offering sweets to little children, to get them into a place where they can sexually assault them)
PEDERASTY	see sodomy	see sodomy
PENIS	the male sexual organ	cock, dick, prick, old fella, john thomas, percy, dong, wang, pecker, willie
PERIOD	the monthly vaginal bleeding by women or adolescent girls	see menstruation
PHALLUS	erect penis	
PORNOGRAPHY	books or films or photos designed to turn people on sexually	porn, stick books
PREGNANT	a woman who has a baby growing in her womb	up the duff, bun in the oven, knocked up, preggers

OFFICIAL NAME	MEANING	SLANG WORDS
PRE-PUBE OR PREPUBESCENT	still a child; not yet at puberty	skinner
PROSTITUTE	someone who has sex for money	hooker, whore (the w is not pronounced), lady of the night, street walker, call girl
PUBERTY	the end of childhood; starting to become sexually mature, as shown by growth of penis and breasts, body hair etc	balls dropping
PUBES	hair around the genitals	fuzz or peachfuzz (for pubes in their first stages of growth)
PUBESCENT	very close to starting puberty	
RAPE	forcing someone to have sex: penis in vagina or anus. Pack rape is rape by a group of men	onion
S&M (sadism and masochism)	sex where people deliberately hurt themselves and each other, for sexual reasons	
SANITARY NAPKIN	pad which is kept in girls underwear to soak up menstrual blood	pad

OFFICIAL NAME	MEANING	SLANG WORDS
SCROTUM	bag of skin which holds the testicles	
SEMEN	white liquid from the penis that carries sperm	cream, white, juice, jizz, cum, spunk
SLUT	girl who has sex with a lot of guys	moll, slag, bike, scruff, tart
SMEGMA	secretion under the foreskin that uncircumcised guys get. Needs to be cleaned away regularly or it becomes smelly	cheese
SODOMY	penis inserted in someone's anus for sexual reasons	buggery, ass-fucking
SPERM	tadpole-like cell produced by man; fertilises ovum to form a baby	
STDs (sexually transmitted diseases)	infections or viruses you can catch by having sex, including herpes, syphilis, gonorrhoea, AIDS	the clap, a dose, the pox
SYPHILIS	see STDs	
TAMPON	small cotton cylinder girls and women use in vagina to soak up blood during their periods	

OFFICIAL NAME	MEANING	SLANG WORDS
TESTICLES/ TESTES	the two organs in the scrotum that make the sperm	balls, nuts
TRANSVESTITE	dressing in the clothes of the other gender	cross-dressing, drag queen
UMBILICAL CORD	cord from the belly-button of a newborn baby, still connecting him to the mother. It is severed after birth	
URETHRA	little hole through which women urinate	
URINE, URINATE	liquid waste, passed through penis or urethra	piss, leak, pee, piddle, number ones, wee
UTERUS	womb	
VAGINA	the passage between the vulva and womb	cunt, hole, twat, slit, fanny, pussy, crack, box, beaver, snatch
VENEREAL DISEASE	see STDs	the clap
VIBRATOR	battery operated object about the size of a penis; used to give sexual excitement	dildo
VIRGIN	someone who's never had sexual intercourse. The word used to be applied only to girls but in recent times	the expression 'taking her cherry' or 'plucking her cherry' means having sex with a virgin

OFFICIAL NAME	MEANING	SLANG WORDS
VIRGIN *(continued)*	has been used for boys also	
VULVA	the lips around the opening of the vagina	
WOMB	the place inside a woman where the unborn baby grows	

GIRLS AND WOMEN

Obviously this is a big topic. But I'll deal briefly with a number of points that might be helpful to you.

There are many things about girls and women that are the same for boys and men, even though that isn't generally recognised. For example, we all know that girls and women are concerned about their bodies: their size and shape, how they look. As discussed earlier, the same applies to boys and men.

With girls and women this concern often leads to big emotional problems.

It's the same for boys and men.

Girls and women often are nervous about relationships, have mixed feelings about sex, lack confidence in dealing with the other sex.

Sound familiar?

In general girls are more likely to talk about relationships and be interested in relationships, are more likely to look for compromises and creative solutions, are more into language, and are more turned on sexually by touch than by sight. But there are so many exceptions to these that it can be quite dangerous to make any generalisations at all. For instance, I'm a male but I'm heavily into language. The idea that women are turned on more by touch might be a social thing, caused by centuries of pressure on women not to have sexual thoughts.

One danger with generalisations about women and girls is that young men might read them and think, 'Oh no, I'm like that too, maybe I'm a girl, or maybe I'm gay.'

These are irrational thoughts.

I'll take the risk though and make a few more comments about girls and women.

For one thing they often have very different relationships with their mother and father than do most boys. For another they often pay more attention to the presentation of their school work. For a third they use their spare time differently.

Again, it's hard to know how much these things go automatically with being female, and how much they are a result of social pressures.

Men and boys often place great store by achievements that can be measured, counted, weighed. So for instance they love to score a century in cricket; considering 100 to be far, far better than 99. They like making money, not necessarily because of what they can do with it, perhaps more because it represents 'points' that they've scored.

A man in a small town in Tasmania told me once that he had 19 children. 'That's amazing', I said. 'Yes,' he replied, 'the bloke on the next farm had 18, and I was determined to keep going till I beat him.'

Women and girls are often more interested in the true nature of the achievement than in the number of 'points' they get.

They certainly use the language of feelings more, but again this could be the result of social pressure. A lot of males would love to talk to a sympathetic listener about their feelings, but they are scared to do so, or they lack the words. When they do talk about feelings it is usually to a female.

Physically girls and boys are very alike until puberty. Puberty can start for girls as young as eight or nine, although that is still unusual. Ten through 12 is average. The first signs are the gradual development of the breasts, starting with breast buds. Breasts and nipples grow. As they grow they can be sore at times, especially if knocked or bumped.

A lot of primary school boys, and even secondary school boys, tease girls about their breast development, or lack of it. Adults may tease them too, and girls may tease other girls. This teasing is extremely dangerous – as it is when boys are teased about their bodies – since it can cause long-term emotional damage.

Many of the people who do this teasing are anxious about their own bodies, or excited or nervous about the appearance of breasts in the girl.

Breasts come in all different shapes and sizes, as do penises, noses, hands, feet, ears, eyebrows; every part of the body.

Boys' genitals change and grow through puberty, and so do girls'. The 'crack' that you see in little girls if you are looking at them from the front widens. It becomes clear that there are in fact two lips which get bigger and more obvious as puberty continues. If you are with a partner who enjoys having you play with her genitals, you'll find that if you part those lips there are two smaller lips inside, between her legs.

At the point where the smaller lips meet at the top of the genitals is a little lump called the clitoris. It has a hood partly covering it. The size of the clitoris varies greatly but the average size is a couple of centimetres. It's often described as a sort of little penis, because it gets stiff when excited, and grows in size. It can give a girl fantastic feelings. In some societies where women are not supposed to enjoy sex, the clitoris is actually cut out from little girls' genitals. This mutilation is called female circumcision, although it's really halfway between circumcision and castration.

Quite a way below the clitoris is the urethra, a tiny hole through which urine comes out. Below that is the much bigger hole, the vagina. The vagina is where the penis enters for sex, where blood comes out during the girl's period, and where babies come out. So it sure is stretchy.

There's a piece of thin skin partly over it, and that's called the hymen. In olden times, and even today in some countries, having an unbroken hymen was a big deal. It was supposed to be proof that the girl was a virgin. As proof it wouldn't get you far in a court of law, as most girls have holes in their hymen even if they are virgins. This can be a result of exercise, masturbation, petting, horse riding, using tampons.

The tearing of the hymen is traditionally supposed to be a cause of great pain, with lots of blood. It can be like that, but for a lot of girls it isn't, and all the stories and jokes can make them unnecessarily scared. However, the first few times they have sex mightn't be terribly enjoyable for some girls. The vagina can take a while to get used to accommodating a penis. If you're a good guy you'll be very patient and careful with a girl who's not used to sex. You'll make sure she's having as good a time as you.

Another change at puberty for girls is of course

the beginning of periods. These start about two years after the breast buds appear. They mightn't start with blood; they might start with a few pale-coloured spots. Gradually the girl settles into a regular cycle.

Every month she'll produce an egg, which buries itself in the lining of the uterus, waiting to be fertilised by the sperm. When she has her period she'll shed less than 30 grams of blood, but it isn't just blood: included in the blood is the egg that wasn't fertilised and the broken-up lining of her uterus, which also wasn't needed that month. Out of every 28 to 35 days a girl will bleed for three to five days.

Girls who bleed heavily will probably use a sanitary napkin: a pad which is kept in their underwear to soak up the blood. Most girls these days use a tampon, which is pushed up into the vagina. A string hangs from the tampon so that the girl can easily remove the tampon when it's time for a new one.

Females don't have periods under the following circumstances:

1. If they're too young or too old.
2. If they're pregnant.
3. Early in adolescence a girl may go for a while without having a period. This just means her body is still getting used to menstruating.

4. Girls who are in full training for sport sometimes stop menstruating.
5. Girls in institutions sometimes stop menstruating. It's almost like with no chance of getting pregnant, the body knows there's no need to menstruate.
6. A girl who is in physical trouble (for example, anorexia), or is on drugs, or on certain medicine, may stop menstruating.

A girl who is about to start her monthly bleeding, or is having her period, can become depressed or bad-tempered or unusually sensitive. This is the famous PMT – pre-menstrual tension. If you're fooling around with one of your friends, and she suddenly snaps angrily at you or runs out of the room crying at something she would have laughed at a few days ago, it may be that she is having her period.

You should be sympathetic in those circumstances, but at the same time she doesn't have the right to insult you just because she's having her period.

Other changes of puberty are similar to the ones guys go through: growth in height and weight, growth of hair, deepening of the voice, the appearance of pimples, greater interest in sex, new ways of thinking, new ambitions.

SOLVING YOUR PROBLEMS

Everyone has problems: men and women, girls and boys. Some people deal with their problems effectively, some don't.

The first thing to know is that when you're upset or angry or depressed, rational thought goes straight out the window. At these times it helps if you recognise you can't always trust your own thoughts.

Here are a few examples:

UPSET THINKING: that teacher's a complete dickhead. He never believes a word I say. He hates my guts.

TRUE THINKING: I don't like him much. Our relationship's been going downhill for a few months now. He's not a very good teacher but I don't put much effort in. If I can't change teachers, if I'm stuck with him, I'd better find some way to work with him, to bring out the best in him.

Here the student may well be showing more maturity than the teacher.

UPSET THINKING: I'll never love anyone the way I love her/him. If she/he doesn't give a stuff about me, there's nothing worth living for.

TRUE THINKING: all moods change eventually. If I can hang in there it will get better. In the meantime maybe I should face up to the fact that I don't have much confidence, and I am pretty lonely. Maybe I should try to do something about those problems. (If the only worthwhile thing in your life is your feeling for this other person, it suggests your life is a bit unbalanced: you need other interests which you find satisfying and important.)

UPSET THINKING: I'll never love anyone the way I love her. Now that she's dropped me, I'm going to make her sorry. For the rest of her life she's going to remember me and mourn for me, and feel bad about how she's treated me.

TRUE THINKING: I'm obsessed with her, and that's not the same thing as love. In fact obsession's got nothing to do with love. I'm actually in a dangerous and self-destructive state. My emotional health is shot. I've lost the plot, big-time. There are people out there who can help me. I'd better find them, fast.

UPSET THINKING: I love her but she's with another guy, or she lives too far away, or she's too old, or I've never even met her, or . . .

TRUE THINKING: I'm not really ready for a serious relationship so I'm having a bit of a fantasy one. The fact is, this girl's not within my 'reach', so I can safely be totally rapt in her, knowing deep down that I'm never going to get on with her.

You may notice in these examples that I'm not suggesting you use any of that self-esteem rubbish: 'BELIEVE IN YOURSELF! YOU CAN DO IT! THINK POSITIVE!'

Anyone who's been seriously depressed or unhappy knows what a waste of time that junk is.

You should recognise however that in some situations depression and being upset may be the right reactions. For example, if your parents separate, if someone close to you dies, if the girl you're rapt in drops you, if you've moved to a new school and don't know anyone, it's entirely natural you'll feel unhappy, maybe terribly unhappy.

Most people think about suicide sometimes. Maybe it's just a passing thought: 'I ought to kill myself, then they'll be sorry.' Some people think about it more strongly. Some people think about it compulsively. Obviously this last one is extremely dangerous. If it describes you, I can make at least one generalisation about you – that you don't feel loved enough by your parents. Whether this is a valid belief doesn't really matter, although I'd guess that it probably is: you probably aren't loved enough. If you were you'd know it. People who are greatly loved don't sit around wondering whether their parents love them.

There's a doctrine in law: *res ipse loquitur*. It means 'the thing speaks for itself'. For example, if a factory has eight serious accidents in six days, the judge may say 'Well, *res ipse loquitur*, I don't need to hear much evidence about this: the factory is clearly unsafe, the facts speak for themselves.'

If you have frequent feelings of depression, distress, lack of confidence, and a desire to commit suicide, this speaks to me of a lack of unconditional love from your parents.

This doesn't mean that they're total write-offs and so too is your relationship with them. There may be lots of good things about you and them. On the other hand there may not be.

So what can you do about your sad feelings?

Well, the golden rule is, talking always helps. There's an important point to make about that though: you have to talk to the right person. For serious problems, the *wrong* people include:

People younger than you
People your own age
People not much older than you
People without imagination
People without understanding
People who go for simple, shallow thinking and simple, shallow solutions
Narrow-minded people
People who have big problems of their own
People who are on drugs

Some of these people don't have enough life experience to give you the best advice. They mean well but it can be quite dangerous acting on their suggestions. Others are too lacking in perspective or wisdom.

Sometimes your parents and other people close to you can be the wrong people too. Why? Because if you need serious long-term help they are too close to give it. Other agendas get in the way. Maybe they are part of the problem, even if you don't yet realise it. Whatever, it is often very difficult for someone to be your parent and your counsellor at the same time.

(Equally it is difficult for a parent to be your teacher. It causes a lot of unnecessary tension.

Some parents, for instance, can teach their sons to drive, or to read better, or to speak another language, but most would be better off not trying.)

To find the right person to talk to, you'll need to look around. Some of the possibilities include teachers, religious leaders, family friends, relatives, doctors, counsellors, psychologists, psychiatrists.

If you're talking to one of them about serious problems you might like to ask before you start whether the things you say will be passed on to anyone else. There may be situations where they will have to take action on something you tell them. It'd be good to have that understood before you start.

Talking is often difficult for guys. Many males have a problem with language and feelings. If your father isn't a talker it might be even harder for you. If you've found the right person to talk to, they'll be good at helping you to talk, at making it easier.

You may make a number of attempts to find someone to talk to, but each time it doesn't work. Perhaps you chose the wrong person. Maybe they do too much talking themselves, and not enough listening. Maybe they give too much advice, instead of helping you make your own decisions. Maybe they spend too much time telling you about their problems. Maybe they're unreliable. Danger signals include phrases like 'I know just how you feel', 'I think you're just feeling sorry for yourself',

'Try thinking about something else for a change', 'You need to eat healthier food', 'Yeah it's like when I broke up with this girl and her mother said I blah blah blah blah blah'. All these approaches are completely unhelpful for dealing with the serious situation in which you find yourself.

If that happens, it doesn't mean you've gone down the wrong road. It just means you chose the wrong person. Try someone else, and keep trying till you find the right person. Don't forget the telephone help-lines, which you'll find at the front of the White Pages, under the heading COMMUNITY HELP REFERENCE PAGE (there's a whole page of them). Most of these are free. In some places they include a Men's Help Line, run by sympathetic and supportive volunteers. There's Lifeline, 24 hours a day, on 13 11 14. There is also The Kids Help Line, 24 hours a day, on 1800 551 800. Most states have a rape crisis line and a domestic violence hotline, both open 24 hours.

If you keep feeling let down by the people you chose, it could of course mean something else: that you're not being honest. Maybe you find the idea of talking to someone about your problems so scary that you keep finding excuses why you can't. You blame them instead of looking at yourself. Maybe you're very nervous about criticising your parents, in case it gets back to them, or because it makes you feel disloyal.

In fact you must find the courage to talk about your relationship with your parents, as well as all the other topics that need exploring. It will be critical that you talk about them; including your positive and negative feelings about them. After all, they are the two most powerful people in your life.

Other ways of reducing depression are largely a matter of common sense. Playing sport, making new friends, meditating, doing something creative. I find that forcing myself to watch comedy videos and comedy TV shows, and reading funny books, can be quite effective.

Isolation is depression's greatest friend. Depression loves it when you shut yourself away from people. It rubs its hands with glee and thinks: 'Beauty! Now I can really mess this guy up!'

Isolation in itself isn't bad – everyone needs to have time on his own, just as he needs to spend time with others – but isolating yourself because you're unhappy or bitter is opening the door wide to depression.

Another tactic for dealing with stress, anxiety, depression is to make an appointment with it.

What it means is that when you're getting stressed, you say to yourself: 'OK, yes, I am hugely stressed about that test or that party or that summons to the principal's office tomorrow, and fair enough too! So what I'll do is make an appointment for the stress. At 11 o'clock this morning, I'll allow myself to feel the full-on stress. I'll take a bath in it, I'll give it everything I've got, I'll cop the full load.'

Then, whenever you feel the stress coming on, you say to it: 'Sorry, you'll have to wait for your appointment. At 11 o'clock you can have all the time and space you want.'

When 11 o'clock comes you postpone the appointment to two o'clock. And so on.

Believe it or not this actually works. Well, it has for me.

The other thing I find helpful is the kind of self-discipline I talked about before, in the section about testing your courage. In particular, not letting your mind go over and over a mistake you've made, torturing yourself by repeating unhelpful abuse like 'How could I have been so stupid!', 'God I'm hopeless', 'I can't believe how dumb I am'.

An old bit of advice says, 'There are three things that can never be recalled: the spent arrow, the thrown stone, the spoken word.'

I do often remind myself of that advice when I've said something especially bad. A few years ago I was at a function where I had to make a speech. I'd been on the road a long time. At the end of the dinner I stood for my speech and began: 'When I arrived here in . . .' I suddenly realised I had no idea of where I was. I had to stop and say to the person next to me: 'Which town am I in?'

He told me, which was kind of him.

It was a pretty rude effort on my part. These people had gone to a lot of trouble to get me there and had planned it for a long time. For the next few days I agonised about it. But there was nothing I could do to cancel my words. They had been spoken, they were out there, people would think whatever they thought, and I couldn't control that or influence it in any way. It was a waste of energy to keep reminding myself of it.

In a situation where you've acted badly – and there will have been plenty already, and there'll be plenty more in the future – work out if there's anything you can do to reduce the damage. A dignified apology for example. (Don't grovel, don't do a suck job, don't lie. A second apology a day or two later, following an apology on the spot, sometimes helps a lot.) An offer to do something practical to help the person. An action in some other area that will show people your feelings about the matter.

If there's nothing you can do, then let it go.

If you commit the same error again soon afterwards, then you'll need to take the famous 'long hard look at yourself'. Sounds to me like you have a problem in this particular area, and you need to work on it before it becomes a bad habit.

Another way of thinking about depression is as

'rage turned inwards'. The anger, fury, despair are inflicted upon yourself. It's like a cancer. It's like the crown of thorns starfish. It's like rust. It eats away inside you, devouring your energy, your good feelings, your sense of reality. You can become depressed, sad, withdrawn.

Some males don't turn their rage inwards: they take it out on people or objects or themselves. These are all inappropriate and unhelpful ways of dealing with it.

It is true that 'bad boys are sad boys'. Boys who act angrily, attacking anyone and everyone, are deeply unhappy, at a level they find frightening to think about. They'll headbutt another player in a football game, give cheek to teachers, start fires, steal, punch their little sister, break windows. Afterwards they'll often burst into tears, beg forgiveness, say, 'I don't know what came over me; I don't know what made me do it.'

It's their sadness that makes them do it, but the terror of facing that is too great for them.

The fact that you're sad is however never an excuse for hurting anyone or anything (including yourself). You have to find the courage to confront your deep unhappiness.

In recent years though I've come to realise that depression, as well as having its awful aspects, can be a kind of gift. It gives you a richer, deeper understanding of your fellow humans. 'You can't appreciate the light until you've known the darkness.' Depression can also give rise to a lot of creative work, like art, music, writing, dance.

BEING UNPOPULAR

Being unpopular is a great fear for many people, adults included. It can have a huge influence on behaviour.

If your fears are realised, and you become unpopular, it's quite a nightmare. Some people reading this book might have been unpopular all their lives. All their school lives anyway.

Sometimes it's a complete rip-off. You're a genuinely decent guy: good-natured, kind, honest, generous. Yet you're the victim of a hard time at school, or elsewhere.

You may be the victim of people who have such stuffed-up personalities that they're taking it out on you. You really are a victim. In this situation you should recruit all the adult help you can. Your own emotional health is very important. Don't put it at risk by going through weeks or months or years of destructive unpopularity.

If someone was breaking the bones in your body one by one, starting at your toes and working their way up your legs, I hope you'd do something about it.

The same applies to emotional damage. The effect is as bad. You must act to stop it.

But it's also possible that you're acting in a way which makes you unpopular. That doesn't alter the fact that you've got to do something. The emotional damage will be as bad even if you're helping cause the problem.

One of the things you can do is figure out why you're unpopular. At least then you're in a position to do something about it, if you want. You might say 'Well, that's the way I am, so stuff them all.' Or you might say: 'Well, that's not too good a habit, so maybe I should change it.'

Among the habits that make people unpopular are:

1. *Talking about yourself all the time*. This can be helped if you get in the habit of asking people about themselves instead – and listening to their answers. People who are good listeners can be very popular indeed.

2. *Exaggerating stuff about yourself, and lying*. This usually means you have a serious problem with confidence. You might need to see a counsellor or someone who's an expert in helping people.

3. *Bragging, or showing off*. Similar to (1) and (2)

above, but not quite the same. You may have parents who are obsessed with you, making you feel that everything you do is incredibly important. If your parents have been telling you that you're a genius or a star or a legend, superior to everyone else, they're not doing you any favours. In fact they're setting you up for a lot of problems. It could also be the opposite: your parents aren't very interested in you. You feel that if you don't draw everyone's attention to what you've achieved, no-one'll notice. (They will; in fact the less you talk about what you've achieved the more they'll notice.)

4. *Talking, or having attitudes, that are more like an adult than someone your age*. A student who is very serious about school work, who doesn't like it when other students 'muck up', who spends more time talking to teachers than students, is in this category. 'You forgot to set any homework,' such a student might say to the teacher, as the rest of the class groan. If this is you, you are probably into control in a big way. You have a lot of fears, and losing control is one of them. Your parents may have put too much emphasis on you being a 'good little boy'. You might have spent too much time with adults, not enough with kids your age mucking

around, lighting your farts or whatever kids in your neighbourhood were doing when you were little. Again a counsellor or someone similar might be needed to help you. Be honest when you talk to them.

5. *Attention seeking behaviour*. This term usually covers a whole lot of stuff, like calling out, insulting other kids, being cheeky to teachers, getting out of your seat in class, or extreme things like breaking windows. True attention seeking behaviour usually means you're scared no-one loves you. Unconsciously you figure at least people will take notice of you if you're acting badly, and that's better than being ignored. If this is you, you've probably been like this for years, and you've probably been in trouble for years. You're going to need to take responsibility for fixing this. Decide which teacher you trust most and start with him. There are strategies available, if you really want to make a change. Beware of labels like A.D.D. or P.T.S.D.: forget the label and look for the individual truth about you. You are a person, not a chapter in a medical book. Again, a good counsellor could be a great idea.

6. *Stealing*. If you steal more than once or twice you are probably seriously unhappy and you

should seek help immediately. Happy well-balanced people don't steal. Another possibility is that you're confused about values: maybe your parents are equally mixed-up about values and have passed on some bad values to you. They could be dishonest, or, even more confusing, they could pose as highly moral and honest people – but you know they do dishonest things.

7. *Being too weak, too quiet, too passive*. You should start working out what you believe in and what you don't. Then stick to your guns. In conversations, give your opinions more, and defend them. Stop trying to please everyone: it's impossible, and you're just setting yourself up for a lifetime of grief. 'I reckon Norths are the biggest thugs in the comp' is more interesting than 'I don't follow any team in particular, I like all of them . . .'

8. *Being selfish with your things, or mean with money*. You've learnt this unattractive behaviour somewhere. Are your parents mean with their things? You might be too fond of being in control, frightened of mess or surprises or people acting wildly. You might be scared that if you give anything away you'll be left with nothing. There's probably been a serious

lack of emotional 'gifts' from your parents to you.

9. *Buying friends*. Again, this suggests a serious problem with confidence, and a relationship with your parents that may look good on the outside but may be very fragile.

10. *Sarcasm, smart comments about other people, gossiping, viciousness, always able to find everyone's weak spots*. This hides massive insecurity. You feel that if you keep attacking everyone, maybe no-one'll get around to attacking you. Your parents have almost certainly picked on you a lot, regularly noting all your faults. You've learnt to despise everyone else. If you're like this, you'll probably deny that you have a problem. You have a lot of work ahead to solve it, but the good news is that it can be done. You'll have to learn to be very honest about yourself – your good points and your bad points – and that's not easy. The interesting thing is you may find it harder to be honest about your good points than your bad points.

11. *Being teacher's pet*. Tough call, because you mightn't have asked for it (although see (4) above). Students often believe all teachers

have 'pets', and no doubt a lot of them do. If you haven't done anything to deserve this honour, and you're sure the teacher is favouring you, try speaking to the teacher outside class time, and explain that it's embarrassing. If you're getting really bad vibes, talk to your parents or a senior teacher you can trust. Don't be afraid to change classes if that's possible and no other solution seems available.

If you are unpopular big-time you should keep in mind the option of changing classes or changing schools. This is entirely reasonable if your emotional health is at risk. But think about changing your behaviour before you start at your new school.

If you've already changed your behaviour at your present school and no-one's giving you credit, then again a change of school might help. It is hard to get rid of a bad reputation. People often take a long time to notice an improvement in someone. It's much easier to get rid of a good reputation.

One last point about friendship and popularity. There's an old saying that you spend your first term at a new school trying to get rid of the friends you made in the first week. Although you may be lonely for a few days when you start a new school it's sometimes not a bad idea to wait a bit before rushing into friendships, so you can see which way the land lies.

THE END

A few years ago I read an article in a Scottish newspaper about the death of a man who had been an international Rugby player. Since he retired from football he'd led a busy life, doing all kinds of things – and very successfully too. Yet when he died, his obituary in the paper was almost all about one event: the fact that 50 years earlier he had acted honestly and generously in a game of football.

> *His first full international, against France, in Paris on January 1 1947, provoked a notable incident: Geddes, in competition with the French wing, pursued a loose ball over his own line and was awarded the touchdown by the referee. However Geddes told the official the Frenchman had been first, with the result that a try was awarded to France who went on to*

> *win 8–3. This sportsmanship made such an impression on the French players that they clubbed together to buy Geddes a cigarette case as a token of their appreciation.*

I was very moved by this. It seemed remarkable to me that at the end of his life, the one thing people remembered about him, the event that made the greatest impression, was the fact that he showed integrity. There was no mention in the article of the great tries Geddes scored, the awards he won, the money he made, or even his career after football.

No, the one thing people concentrated on was that under enormous pressure he was honest in a game of Rugby.

Perhaps this is the way that you would like to be remembered. As a decent, honest person, a man of integrity. A man of whom it can be said:

'You can trust him.'

'He won't let you down.'

'There's no bullshit about him.'

'He's always got a good word for everyone.'

'Ask him; he won't stuff you around.'

'If he tells you he'll do something, it'll be done.'

These are fine words to be said of anyone. If you hear people speak of you in these terms then there's a pretty fair chance that you're on the way to becoming an adult.

A man.

John Marsden

Tomorrow, When the War Began

Hell isn't only a place for the damned, sometimes it's a place where the saved take refuge.

Seven teenagers take a trip to Hell.

And seven come back. To Hell.

Get ready. This is real. This is true.

What will you do tomorrow?

The first book in the most powerful series ever written for young Australians.

'The reader is unwittingly flung headlong and gasping into the plot . . . the images created are so vivid that they stay with you long after the book is reluctantly closed on the final page'
HERALD SUN

'This is a story to be read at full pelt – I could not put it down – and then returned to, for a second and third more thoughtful savouring'
AUSTRALIAN BOOKSELLER & PUBLISHER

'This is an enlightening book about growing up and discovering who you are'
SUNDAY TELEGRAPH

John Marsden

The Dead of the Night

It's tough surviving in Hell.

But sometimes Hell can be a haven.

Australia has been invaded. Nothing is as it was. Six teenagers are living out their nightmare in the sanctuary of a hidden valley, making their own rules, protecting what's theirs, struggling for courage in a world changed forever.

But sometimes courage demands too high a price . . .

Intense, passionate, and compulsive . . . the frighteningly real story begun in *Tomorrow, When the War Began* continues.

'This is a war story told with storytelling skills that Alistair Maclean used to display . . . I found reading this book a breatholding experience'
VIEWPOINT

'. . . the very best kind of war story . . . this is sensitive and moving writing'
AUSTRALIAN BOOK REVIEW

'. . . one of those rare sequels that sustains the standard of its predecessor . . . for adult devotees as well as discerning teenagers'
HERALD SUN

John Marsden
The Third Day, the Frost

What's the biggest danger you can think of?
This is bigger.

What's the toughest challenge you can imagine?
This is tougher.

What's the greatest fear you have?
You're about to find out.

First there was *Tomorrow, When the War Began*, then came *The Dead of the Night*. Now it's *The Third Day, the Frost*. And things can only get worse . . .

The breathtaking sequel to *Tomorrow, When the War Began* and *The Dead of the Night*.

'This is real *Day of the Jackal* stuff and, if you want action, adventure and heart-stopping danger, *The Third Day, the Frost* delivers'
SYDNEY MORNING HERALD

'Tense, exciting and, most importantly, realistic. I wish I could read this series again for the first time'
SUN-HERALD

'. . . is this really the kids' last outing? We're going to miss them. Bestseller material'
AUSTRALIAN BOOKSELLER & PUBLISHER

John Marsden

Darkness, Be My Friend

That's what war does for you. Either kills you in one hit or destroys you slowly. One way or the other, it gets you.

Unless you fight back.

Darkness, Be My Friend continues the story of the multi-award winning *Tomorrow, When the War Began* series.

'This is a book that is hard to put down. It's grim, it's conscious-raising, it's gripping in its intensity and its intrigue. It's Marsden at his best!'
GEELONG ADVERTISER

'Again it's a Marsden triumph, an exhilarating mix of raw courage and blinding fear . . .'
THE MERCURY

'Each book has its place in the tone and tenor of the series, but *Darkness, Be My Friend* is one of the best . . . Like ancient myths, the stories confront the purpose of life, death, betrayal, killing, love, hate, revenge, selflessness, sacrifice and, in this most recent book, faith.'
THE AGE

John Marsden
Burning for Revenge

The tips of the fingers on my right hand had gone beyond extreme pain. I couldn't feel them properly any more. I knew they were still digging in, but I knew they couldn't dig in any longer.

My left hand kept scanning. And connected with something. Not much. By God, it wasn't much – some sort of metal pin. All I knew was that it was metal and it wasn't a regular shape. There was a hard solid bit, then some wire.

It wasn't much to stake my life on. But I had nothing else. There wasn't enough to hold on to, or to get my hand around. All I could do was use it as a springboard. Something to push against, to give me the resistance for one last leap at the top.

One last leap at life.

They're back.

While trying to hold together their lives and relationships, they also have to cope with the enemy. An enemy which has penetrated everywhere. An enemy growing more dangerous, more skilful, by the day.

Roaring back into action, Ellie and Homer lead the single most daring raid of the entire war.

Burning for Revenge is the sensational fifth title in the *Tomorrow, When the War Began* series.

John Marsden
Dear Miffy

'You can squeeze my lemon baby, juice runs down my legs.'

Sex, I can't stop thinking about it but. It's like the best sweetest torture ever invented. It tears you apart but you wouldn't want it any other way. It's the drug you never try to give up . . .

Tony writes letters.
To Miffy.
And breaks your heart.

Is there something wrong when your main ambition in life is to be dead?

John Marsden
Everything I Know About Writing

The ultimate 'get off your bum and do it' book, *Everything I Know About Writing* will motivate anyone to write. It's a lively funny guide to writing, as readable as a novel, but packed from front to back with ideas and insights.

And this new edition has one other very special feature: nearly 600 extraordinary topics, guaranteed to have you or your students writing before you know it.

John Marsden is not just one of Australia's most successful writers of all time; he's also one of our best teachers of writing. *Everything I Know About Writing* is the most painless way into writing – ever.

'. . . highly recommended . . .'
SUN-HERALD, Sydney

'. . . the most exciting, interesting and useful book on the teaching of writing . . . *Everything I Know About Writing* is a must . . .'
AUSTRALIAN ENGLISH TEACHER